Implied Trusts and Beneficial Ownership in Modern UK Tax Law

by
Chris Thorpe

First published January 2022

Reprinted (with amendments), March 2023

by Spiramus Press Ltd

102 Blandford Street

London W1U 8AG

www.spiramus.com

© Spiramus Press Ltd

ISBN

9781913507381 Paperback

9781913507398 Digital

British Library Cataloguing-in-Publication Data.

A catalogue record for this book is available from the British Library.

The right of Chris Thorpe to be identified as the author of this work has been asserted by him in accordance with the Copyright, Designs and Patents Act, 1988.

Printed and bound in Great Britain by Grosvenor Group (Print Services) Ltd

To my children Eleanor and Thomas Thorpe

About the author

Chris is a Fellow of the Chartered Institute of Taxation and full member of the Society of Trust & Estate Practitioners, having originally qualified as a barrister. He qualified as a tax advisor at Grant Thornton and has worked in private practice and as a lecturer.

Contents

List of abbreviations

CA 2006	Companies Act 2006
CAA 2001	Capital Allowances Act 2001
CTA 2009	Corporation Tax Act 2009
CTA 2010	Corporation Tax Act 2010
FA 2021 etc.	Finance Acts
ICTA 1970	Income and Corporation Taxes Act 1970
ICTA 1988	Income and Corporation Taxes Act 1988
IHTA 1984	Inheritance Tax Act 1984
ITA 2007	Income Tax Act 2007
ITEPA 2003	Income Tax (Earnings and Pensions) Act 2003
ITTOIA 2005	Income Tax (Trading and Other Income) Act 2005
TCGA 1992	Taxation of Chargeable Gains Act 1992
TMA 1970	Taxes Management Act 1970

Table of authorities

Cases

CONTENTS

Statutes

Introduction

There is no shortage of literature, commentary and case law concerning implied trusts nor of the legal and equitable principles which bring them about (e.g. proprietary estoppel); however, there is very little about their place within the UK tax system. The literature tends to focus on the mechanisms of the trust and the proprietary rights of the various parties; but few examine His Majesty's Revenue & Customs' (HMRC) attitude, understanding and approach to such trusts and the treatment and imposition of beneficial ownership. It is not just HMRC's understanding and treatment of beneficial ownership and its imposition via implied trusts which is scarcely addressed, it is also that of the tax courts and legislation. It is a critical question because a government can only tax income and capital assets which belong to someone; so, to whom does it belong? Often it is not the person whose name is listed as the 'legal owner', but the person listed as the 'beneficial owner'. An implied trust will then impose that beneficial ownership upon anyone other than the legal owner in accordance with equitable principles.

Some of the tax statutes discuss beneficial ownership and the basis of that degree of ownership of an asset for taxing individuals and trustees, but there are inconsistencies in places. Beneficial ownership is not universally addressed in all areas of tax throughout the legislation. The long-standing pieces of legislation which bring together the concept of beneficial ownership and implied trusts are the settlements legislation and that concerning the Transfer of Assets Abroad (TOAA) rules, both of which effectively impose implied trusts so that the 'real' owner of the asset is taxed accordingly. New legislation was also introduced in April 2009 addressing transfers of income streams between individuals. In none of these pieces of legislation is there any mention of implied trusts specifically or even of equity. Of these, this book will focus primarily on the settlements legislation and its development.

This book will also explore those areas of modern UK tax law (represented by the courts, the legislation and the executive) to discover the importance of beneficial ownership and how it took root therein; it will pull these threads together. Implied trusts are central to this theme of where beneficial ownership lies and this book looks at some important aspects: what these trusts are, where they came from, why and how they are applied and recognised by the three arms of modern UK tax law, and what their place is in legal history.

INTRODUCTION

It is important to note that whilst the title of this book concerns UK tax law, it will be focusing more specifically upon that of England & Wales. Whilst the tax laws are almost universal throughout the UK, Scotland and Northern Ireland do have their own judicial systems and courts; and whilst the tax tribunals have jurisdiction across all the UK, these nations have their own higher courts. In particular, Scotland has a form of unitary ownership whereby only legal ownership is recognised. Whilst trust law does exist in Scotland, the significance of beneficial ownership and implied trusts does not permeate through Scots law as it does through that of England and Wales.

1 What is beneficial ownership?

"It was as true…as taxes is. And nothing's truer than them" [1]

A beneficial or 'equitable' owner is a person who actually owns and enjoys an asset – not necessarily the same person whose name is recorded as the official or legal owner. It is called 'beneficial' simply because that person has the benefit or use of it. More than that though, beneficial owners might be the owner, in reality, because they paid for the asset or produced the income to pay for it, common law and officialdom merely placed the label of owner on someone else. The common law only recognises official ownership and did not give regard to who might be the person who paid for or benefited from it in reality; equity recognises real ownership in substance, not just in official title. This is summed up by Eyre CB in the case of *Dyer v. Dyer*:[2]

> *"…. the trust of a legal estate, whether freehold, copyhold, or leasehold; whether taken in the names of the purchasers and other jointly, or in the names of others without that of the purchaser; whether in the one name or several; whether jointly or successive - results to the man who advances the purchase-money".*

When the legal and beneficial ownership of an asset is split between two different people then, by definition, a trust is formed. If the different ownership is written down (or at least deliberately and expressly-stated) then it is an 'express' trust. Otherwise, beneficial ownership will have to be 'implied' by the courts. The legislation recognises this, the prime examples being the settlements legislation and that for TOAA, both of which impose beneficial ownership by the effective creation of an implied trust, as does relatively-recent legislation in ITA 2007 chapter 5A addressing the disposal of income streams by individuals[3]. The Judicature Acts of 1873-75 (and later, Senior Court Acts 1981 s.49) decreed that equity (and thus the concept of beneficial ownership) takes priority over legal ownership; HMRC acknowledges this supremacy through guidance and instruction to its staff and Inspectors, and the courts have done the same.

Beneficial ownership is a very topical issue of late and certainly does not just belong in the Middle Ages or Victorian times. In January 2020, the EU's 5th Anti Money-Laundering Directive (5AMLD) became law in the UK. This is

---

[1]Charles Dickens, *David Copperfield*, ch. 19

[2](1788) 2 Cox Eq Cas 92

[3] ITA 2007 sections 809AZA-809AAZB which applies to transfers on or after 22 April 2009 and for which similar rules exist for corporate transferors

discussed later, but the essence of this change is that all UK trusts (even bare trusts) will be required to report to HMRC and disclose the identity of the beneficial owners. This, together with the earlier 4th Anti Money-Laundering Directive (4AMLD, which came into force in 2017) has had a revolutionary effect on trust law. The legal owner of an asset has always been known to the outside world, with the beneficial ownership known only to those party to a trust. To shine a spotlight onto those beneficial owners is a huge step away from historical official recognition of only legal ownership. This change overturns centuries of the common-law approach of identifying and recognising only the legal owners. This has also been relevant for limited companies as well as trusts; companies have to disclose their beneficial ownership through the register of Persons of Significant Control (PSC) i.e. who actually owns this business and not just whose name is on the share register at Companies House.

So, if beneficial ownership is not defined and laid down elsewhere in statute or common law, what authority does the law have to impose it on someone other than the official owner? The answer lies in the laws of conscience.

2 What is an implied trust?

> *"If it is intended to have a resulting trust, the ordinary and familiar mode of doing that is by saying so on the face of the instrument; and I cannot get, out of the language of this instrument, a resulting trust except by putting in words which are not there"* [1]

This quote from *Smith v. Cooke* above gives us a clue about the starting position of defining an implied trust (a 'resulting' trust in particular). There is no written instrument outlining where the ownership is to lie, so the courts write the words into an imaginary deed in accordance with the parties' intentions or the rules of common law or principles of fairness and equity. They are essentially in place to right a wrong or recognise a form of ownership which was not acknowledged under common law.

In the creation of this implied trust, the strict legal position is effectively ignored with the legal owner will be given the title of trustee, with the one who advances the purchase money (i.e. the person who effectively, practically and beneficially owns the asset) being the beneficiary. The type of implied trust in this scenario would be a resulting trust, as discussed below. The practice of overlooking a legal owner toward the actual owner (in all but name) was well established by the time *Dyer v. Dyer* was heard in the old Exchequer Court.

Cook v. Fountain [2] laid down the modern distinction between the 'express' and 'implied' ('resulting' or 'constructive') trusts in 1676:

> *"All trusts are either, first, express trusts, which are raised and created by act of the parties, or implied trusts, which are raised or created by act or construction of law; again, express trusts are declared either by word or writing; and these declarations appear either by direct or manifest proof, or violent and necessary presumption. These are commonly called presumptive trusts; and that is, when the court, upon consideration of all circumstances presumes there was a declaration, either by word or writing; though the plain and direct proof thereof be not extant. In the case in question there is no pretence of any proof that there was a trust declared either by word or in writing; so the trust, if there be any, must either be implied by the law, or presumed by the court"* [3]

---

[1] Per Lord Halsbury LC in *Smith v. Cooke* [1891] AC 297 at 299

[2] (1676) 3 Swans at 585

[3] Ibid at 591

Trusts (of a kind) were being used in classical times; Roman civil law contained the concept of 'fiducia', a relationship of good faith over the strict letter of the law, using the 'fideicommissum' - the closest relative to the modern trust. However, UK trust law as we recognise it today is traceable back to the times of the crusades. The early equity courts had formed the concept of 'feoffee of use' who would hold the legal titles of properties of knights in the Holy Land, the latter being the 'cestui que use' or later 'cestui que trust' i.e. the beneficiary. Henry VIII's Statute of Uses in 1536 effectively signalled the beginning of modern formal trusts by abolishing the informal (and often abusive) 'uses' which based ownership upon possession (or 'seisin'). By the early 17th century, the courts had established the principle of imposed implied trusts for executors holding un-disposed estate residue for beneficiaries. [4] Later, the *Earl of Oxford's case*[5] resulted in the issuing of an injunction prohibiting the execution of a common law order, establishing the concept that equity can potentially take precedence over established common law. The 1873 and 1875 Judicature Acts cemented that precedence of equity as well as giving us the civil courts structure which we see today.

Constructive trusts are traditionally those imposed by law following an act of fraud or wrongdoing. In more modern times the constructive trust has become an available tool of the equitable/restorative concept of proprietary estoppel whereby a promise, relied upon by someone to their detriment and has been reneged upon, can be enforced; the unfortunate person who relied upon that promise can be given a beneficial proprietary stake in the property in question.

The imposition of an implied trust was traditionally a last resort. In *Cook v. Fountain*, Lord Nottingham said: [6]

> *"The law never implies and the court never presumes a trust, but in case of absolute necessity. The reason for this rule is sacred; for if the Chancery do take the liberty to construe a trust by implication of law, or to presume a trust unnecessarily, a way is open to the Lord Chancellor to construe or presume any man in England out of his estate"*

The existence of trusts had relied upon there being proof that the trust had been created or the facts admitted. Following the Statute of Frauds,[7] in the

---

[4]*Brereton v. Roberts* (1608-09) Tothill 87

[5](1615) 21 ER 485

[6](1676) 3 Swans at 592

[7](29 Car 2 c 3) (1677)

IMPLIED TRUSTS

year after *Cook v. Fountain*, the existence of express trusts became more prominent. The Statute required trusts of land to be conveyed in writing but exempted 'resulting' and 'constructive' trusts from that criterion.

So, what are resulting and constructive trusts?

2.1 Resulting trusts

The first type of resulting trust is the 'presumed intention' resulting trust, which are imposed by courts in the manner laid down in *Dyer v. Dyer*. They look at the presumed intentions of the parties and bring them to fruition e.g. that the person who advanced the money is the true owner and as such should be the beneficiary of that property held in trust by the trustee. This would be achieved on the presumption that the parties always intended it to be thus, and that the official title just happened to lie with the legal purchaser. This trust would therefore look at the intentions of the parties involved and the making of presumptions regarding gifts. Lindley LJ summed it up in the case of *Standing v Bowring* when he stated:

> "*Trusts are neither created nor implied by law to defeat the intentions of donors or settlors; they are created or implied or are held to result in favour of donors or settlors in order to carry out, and give effect to their true intentions, expressed or implied*"[8]

This presumption is not new (per Lord Nottingham in *Cook v. Fountain*, cited above). Lord Nottingham's presumptive trust came to an end in 1677 with the Statute of Frauds (which Lord Nottingham helped draft) and which stated that any declaration of trust must be in writing. This led, according to Chambers, to the effective creation of a presumption of trust/declaration, rather than intention itself based primarily on the lack of consideration. It is that a gift has been made for no consideration and at the donor's expense with no obvious explanation, and so a question mark arises over it. Chambers broadly (sub)categorises this as:

(a) voluntary conveyance, and

(b) purchase-money resulting trusts

"*the problem is the same in both: it appears that one person has been enriched at the expense of another and there is no explanation for it*".[9]

Lord Upjohn pointed out that:

---

[8] (1885) 3 Ch D 282 (CA) at 289

[9] In his essay in "*Constructive and Resulting Trusts*" at page 268

> *"the presumption of a resulting trust is no more than a long stop to provide the answer when the relevant facts and circumstances fail to yield a solution"*[10]

Chambers was rather scathing about the existence of these initial presumptions of a resulting trust, pointing out that the courts have frequently found the 'relevant facts' on the slimmest of evidence and concludes that *"we do not need the presumptions and would be better off without them"*[11]. Chambers, along with Swadling, subscribes to the view that all resulting trusts are essentially tools against unjust enrichment, similar to the traditional constructive trust. The modern constructive trust now takes up the role of enforcing presumed intentions between parties – evidenced by the many cases concerning family homes and the common intention to share that home even though only one of the couple had purchased it. There is some arguably some overlap between these presumed intentions resulting and modern constructive trusts.

The second type of resulting trust is the 'automatic' one. These take the Latin word *resalire* (to 'rebound' or 'spring back') more literally by placing the ownership of a failed gift back into the hands of the original donor – the beneficial ownership is *"never drawn off him"*.[12] The gift has failed, so the trust is not so much based on the presumed intention of the parties, but more a remedial tool. The automatic resulting trust is borne primarily from the failure of an express trust when the title to the property remains with the settlor of the trust who has failed to effectively dispose of his property and fulfils the equitable maxim of *"equity abhors a vacuum"* (i.e. someone must own the property).

The classic explanation, and indeed the origin of the description 'automatic resulting trust' was laid down by Megarry J:

> *"the transfer to B is made on trusts which leave some or all of the beneficial interest undisposed of. Here B automatically holds on a resulting trust for A to the extent that the beneficial interest has not been carried to him or others"*[13]

We therefore have this dividing line within resulting trusts between those that operate on the presumption of the parties, and the 'automatic' resulting

---

[10]In *Vandervell v. IRC* [1967] 2 AC 291 at 313

[11]At page 270 in his essay in *"Constructive and Resulting Trusts"*

[12]*Godbold v. Freestone* (1695) 3 Lev 406

[13]*Re Vandervell's Trusts (No.2)* [1974] Ch 269 at 294

trusts which appear to operate as a matter of law because a transfer (or express trust) has failed. The neatest summing up on resulting trusts and the varying roles they play (and the various theories behind them), is found within Edwin Simpson's essay[14] on resulting trusts where he says:

> "One proposed unifying theory is that all resulting trusts give effect to the presumed intention of the transferor of property (which he refers to as the orthodox view). The other, that they arise because the transferor had no actual intention to benefit its recipient (which he calls the 'restitutionary' view put forward by Prof Birks and Dr Chambers). The third stance, that there can be no unifying theory at all, holds that the "apparent gift" instances depend upon a presumed intention, whilst the "failed disposition" cases arise automatically, or as it is sometimes put, by operation of law"

According to Jennifer Payne[15] it was the *Westdeutsche*[16] decision which brought into the fold of resulting trusts the scenario whereby a sum of money is advanced from A to B for a specific purpose, but before that purpose is fulfilled B goes bankrupt and the money is not held in B's estate but in trust for A. This was the broad issue within the House of Lords case of *Barclays Bank v. Quistclose Investments Ltd.*[17] This would have been categorised in Megarry J's category of automatic resulting trusts until Lord Browne-Wilkinson in *Westdeutsche* effectively held that all resulting trusts are presumed intention – whether that intention stems from holding property in the name of another or that the settled property should return to the donor in so far as he has failed to dispose of it effectively:

> "Under existing law a resulting trust arises in two sets of circumstances: (A) where A makes a voluntary payment to B or pay (wholly or in part) for the purchase of property which is vested in either B alone or in the joint names of A and B, there is a presumption that A did not intend to make a gift to B: the money or property is held on trust for A or in the case of a joint purchase by A and B in shares proportionate to their contributions....(B) where A transfers property to B on express trust, but the trusts declared do not exhaust the whole beneficial interest"

---

[14]In his essay "On the Nature of Resulting Trusts: the Vandervell Litigation Revisited" cited in "Restitution & Equity Volume 1 – Resulting Trusts and Equitable Compensations"

[15]In her essay within "Restitution & Equity Volume 1" page 77-79

[16]Westdeutsche Landesbank Girozentrale v. Islington BC [1996] 2 AC 669

[17][1970] AC 567

It was precisely this dividing line which Edwin Simpson pointed out as the third stance.

John Mee[18] briefly discusses the theory that these automatic resulting trusts are essentially tools of restitution – an idea initially put forward by Peter Birks who also wrote several articles on constructive trusts' being a tool to remedy unjust enrichment, so the partial overlap of the two types of implied trust comes through. P J Millett too looked at the use of both constructive and resulting trusts in such a manner.[19] But the main difference between the two types of trust was described in his book *Unjust Enrichment*[20] as a *"concealed synonym of restitutionary in the unextended sense in which it was confined to giving back. A resulting benefit is one returning whence it came"*. Dr Chambers too argues that the concept of restitution underlies all resulting trusts insofar as *"the provider of the property did not intend to benefit the recipient"*.[21] This is something to which Mee refers, citing Swalding who had criticised the very title 'automatic' – *"there's nothing automatic about the law, the resulting trust does not arise of its own volition, but because the courts say it does.*[22] Why, he asks, should a new trust arise out of the ashes of a failed one? Edwin Simpson, when discussing *Re Vandervell's Case (No.2)*[23] seems to suggest that the distinction between the presumed intention and automatic resulting trust is also somewhat artificial in that both are products of the law rather than any directly evidenced intention by the parties:

> *"Neither trust simply gives effect to a sufficiently manifested intention that the property should be so held. Each arises by virtue of a legal operation, rather than by virtue of a legal recognition of the effectiveness of an individual's sufficiently manifested will in respect of the disposition of his own property"*[24]

I would agree with this suggestion. In *Westdeutsche*, Lord Browne-Wilkinson drew that faint line between 'presumed intention' (circumstance 'A', from above) and 'automatic' resulting trusts (circumstance 'B') and clearly there

---

[18]In his essay in Mitchell's *"Constructive and Resulting Trusts"*

[19]Restitution and Constructive Trusts 1998 LJR 399

[20]2nd Ed OUP 2004 at 304

[21]R Chambers, *"Resulting Trusts"* as cited in John Mee's essay in *"Constructive and Resulting trusts"* page 221

[22]Ibid at page 210

[23][1974] Ch 269

[24]Edwin Simpson "On the nature of resulting trusts: The Vandervell Litigation Revisited". Cited in *Restitution & Equity Volume 1*

IMPLIED TRUSTS

are different types of trusts for different circumstances. There are those scenarios (which I will call '*Dyer v Dyer*' scenarios) whereby assumptions are made about the parties' intentions – person A buying a property but on behalf of himself and person B, who contributed some of the purchase funds. This would be a 'presumed intention' trust clearly; if person A were asked whether they were buying the property purely for himself, he would reply in the negative – he was buying it for both of them. That is an operation of law, as Simpson explains, but it is the law of equity and conscience which is doing so in the name of the parties' presumed intention. An 'automatic' resulting trust is an operation of the same law, but not in line with the parties' intention, rather the transfer of property from person A to person B was simply not properly executed. This '*Vandervell*' scenario (these cases are described in more detail below) is more of a corrective action, rather than one based on intention. This has many traits of the constructive trust, acting as a tool of restitution or fail-safe, to ensure that a transaction isn't left incomplete.

Ultimately, whether it is labelled 'presumed intention' or 'automatic', these trusts achieve the same thing, namely: returning the beneficial interest of an asset to the original owner.

Having looked into the subtle differences between the two types of resulting trusts and their modern interpretation, we start to merge with the 'new model constructive trust'. This was something which Lord Denning MR had described as being the "*latest progeny of equity…that was not past its child-bearing age*" and had been brought into the world by Lord Diplock.[25] This new model constructive trust started to base itself upon the presumed intentions and set itself up as a weapon in the hands of the equitable concept of proprietary estoppel – that the conduct of the parties meant it would be inequitable to deny the beneficiary use of the property as it went against their clear presumption which is equitable in the circumstances. Here too is another area of overlap between resulting and constructive trusts; but now the common ground is not restitution, rather common or presumed intention with the 'new model' or 'reliance-based' modern constructive trusts in this role of correcting a perceived wrong.

---

[25]*Eves v. Eves* [1975] 1 WLR 1338 at 1341 referring to Lord Diplock's statement in *Gissing v. Gissing* [1971] AC 886 at 905

2.2   Constructive trusts

The basis of the 'traditional' constructive (derived from the word *'construe'*) trust has nothing to do with presumed intention and can be summed up nicely by Donovan Waters:[26]

> *"there is such a wide range of conflicting judicial and academic views, both as to the nature and the importance of the constructive trust in English law, that it is difficult to find two people who are in complete agreement. All the same, there is one point upon which all would agree. It is at least accepted by courts and theorists <u>that this trust is imposed by law, and that the intention of the parties, whom it affects, it consequently irrelevant</u>".*

In setting out his stall for the English constructive trust being a remedy (as it has traditionally been in the United States) rather than merely a substantive institution, he later described it as *"unlike a trust intended by the parties, is machinery only"*.[27] It is therefore unlike the resulting trust (the 'presumed intention' resulting trust certainly) in that it is based solely upon a construal of the legislation and is simply a remedy (in Waters' view) to any breach thereof.

The traditional constructive trust also revolves around the relevant parties' relationship being a fiduciary one. An early example of a constructive trust can be traced back to 1579 when the concept of constructive notice was imposed on vendors of leases who knowingly bought land, the freehold to which had already been bought.[28] Underhill & Hayton[29] list the headings when a constructive trust may be imposed by law:

i.   *"On the profits of a breach of fiduciary duty*
ii. *On trust property transferred to third parties in breach of trust*
iii. *On profits of wrongdoing*
iv. *To prevent the fraudulent or unconscionable invocation of legal rules to deny the claimant's right to property* (under which they include common intention constructive trusts and proprietary estoppel)
v.   *On property that is subject to a specifically enforceable contract of sale*
vi. *In response to unjust enrichment"*

---

[26]"The Constructive Trust: the case for a new approach in English law" page 1

[27]Ibid at page 8

[28]*Ireby v. Gibone* (1579) Cary 82-83

[29]"*Law of Trust & Trustees*". Chapter 9

With considerable overlap, Paul Matthews[30] lists his instances when a constructive trust will arise:

    i.   *Trusts created by statute (e.g. co-ownership of land under Law of Property Act 1925 sections 34 and 36)*

    ii.   *Where an express trust passes trust property to a successor trustee*

    iii.   *Where an express trustee pockets trust property for himself*

    iv.   *Void distributions to beneficiaries*

    v.   *Where trust property is alienated in breach of trust to a third party who is not a bona fide purchaser for value of legal estate without notice*

    vi.   *Fruits of trust property*

    vii.   *Tracing into proceeds of express trust property*

    viii.   *Property which a trustee has a duty not to get for himself*

    ix.   *Specifically enforceable contracts for the transfer of property rights*

    x.   *Mutual wills*

    xi.   *Proprietary estoppel*

    xii.   *Common intention constructive trusts*

The last two of these, in particular, deviate from the traditional model and rely on Lord Denning's latest progeny of equity: being used to remedy equitable wrongs rather than legal ones.

In line with the theme of equitable courts, the versatility of constructive trusts has been commented upon by the highest courts:

> *"English law provides no clear and all-embracing definition of a constructive trust. Its boundaries have been left perhaps deliberately vague, so as not to restrict the court by technicalities in deciding what the justice of a particular case may demand".[31]*

Another interesting example of a constructive trust's versatility is with 'secret trusts'. These arise when A dies leaving property to B, but only after an undertaking by B that he will hold the property on trust for C. According to Simon Gardner[32], these posthumous trusts are indeed constructive trusts and are able to avoid the formalities of the Wills Act 1837 surrounding testamentary dispositions for the simple reason that they are not dispositions upon death; rather, they are trusts formed after death. He puts them into the context of a traditional constructive trust:

> *"the law imposes a constructive trust in such a way as to produce an outcome which someone intended and which would not otherwise come about. For*

---

[30]In his essay in "Constructive and Resulting Trusts pages 4 and 5"

[31]*Carl Zeiss Stiftung v. Herbert Smith (No.2)* [1969] 2 Ch 276 at page 300 per Edmund Davies LJ

[32]In his essay in Mitchell's "Constructive and Resulting Trusts"

example, a secret trust tracks the testator's informally expressed wishes for the post-mortem disposition of his property"[33]

A common example of when HMRC will recognise a constructive trust is upon the declaration of an unlawful (or *ultra vires*) dividend e.g. because of insufficient distributable reserves, by a limited company when the shareholder knew, or had reasonable grounds to suspect, this was the case. According to their guidance:

"A 'constructive' trust is imposed by law in certain circumstances that the law 'construes' (interprets) as requiring the legal owner of property in good conscience not to retain all beneficial interest in it… It can also apply in the tax context of an unlawful dividend where the shareholder receiving the dividend holds it as 'constructive trustee' for the company".[34]

And:

"Where a dividend is ultra vires (in whole or part) and the shareholder knew or had reasonable grounds to believe that the dividend was unlawful (as normally would be the case where the shareholder is also a director) then the shareholder receiving the dividend, or that part of it, holds it as constructive trustee….A shareholder who had no knowledge of the illegality of the dividend and no reasonable grounds in which so to believe is not a constructive trustee". [35]

This guidance reminds us not only of an occasion when a constructive trust may be imposed, but also the relevance of the defaulter's knowledge of the wrongdoing. One basic criterion of the law of conscience is that it will only intervene when someone's conscience is malevolent or reckless; the references above refer to 'good conscience' and the shareholder's knowing that the dividend was unlawful thus holding those monies on trust for the company. If someone acts in good faith, then no constructive trusteeship can be imposed upon them. With equity's having conscience at its core, any remedial tool will therefore revolve around the parties' intentions and conduct to some degree, thus highlighting the similarities with presumed intention resulting trusts.

The constructive trust has thus evolved into a tool to remedy equitable wrongs based upon the intentions (and conduct) of the parties, and thus carry out the bidding of a representational estoppel which, according to

---

[33]Ibid page 63

[34]HMRC guidance TSEM9705

[35]HMRC guidance CTM15205

Matthews,[36] was given the name 'proprietary estoppel' in 1966 in the 26th edition of *Snell's Equity*. The phrase 'common-intention constructive trust' then appeared later in David Hayton's 1988 book *"Remedial Constructive Trusts of Homes: An Overseas View"*, making its first court appearance in *Mollo v. Mollo*[37] in 1999.

The standard starting point for this type of trust is the Lord Diplock statement in *Gissing v. Gissing*:[38]

> *"a resulting, implied or constructive trust – and it is unnecessary for present purposes to distinguish between these three classes of trust – is created by a transaction between the trustee and the cestui-que trust in connection with the acquisition by the trustee of a legal estate in land, whenever the trustee has so conducted himself that that it would be inequitable to allow him to deny to the cestui-que trust a beneficial interest in the land acquired... and he will be held to have conducted himself if by his words or conduct he has induced the cestui-que trust to act to his own detriment in the reasonable belief that by so acting he was acquiring a beneficial interest in the land"*

As an aside, it is interesting that in his statement, Lord Diplock distinguished resulting and constructive trusts from implied trusts. Lords Reid, Morris and Dilhorne said the same several times within their judgments in *Gissing v. Gissing*. Maybe they regard resulting and constructive trusts purely as tools of equity, designed to remedy a particular issue in a particular circumstance; with implied trusts merely recognising an existing state of affairs. It is a pity that Lord Diplock did not go into more detail as to the distinction. Maybe it was their view that the three trusts could be presented together as merely variations on a theme, the finer distinctions between them being irrelevant; after all, they produce the same outcome in practical terms, with equitable principles at their core however they are manifested.

Matthews points out that this concept of proprietary estoppel was actually nothing new.[39] The common intention in this case being merely evidentiary to the common intention behind the trust – *"common intention showed the intention to induce reliance. Bingo".*[40] There is arguably some overlap between the equitable concept and the constructive trust imposed to enforce the

---

[36]In his essay in "Constructive and Resulting Trusts" at page 24

[37][1999] EGCS 117

[38][1971] AC 886

[39] In *Dillwyn v. Llewelyn* (1862) 4 De GF & J 517

[40] Paul Matthew's essay in *"Constructive and Resulting Trusts"* page 50

justice, the outcome of the trust being the rationale behind the estoppels; the well-known statement in *Yaxley v. Gotts*[41] where Walker LJ stated that the two concepts coincide is an example of this. But Lord Walker reminded us in *Stack v. Dowden*[42] that the estoppel is a *"mere equity....asserting an equitable claim against the conscience of the true owner"* ...whereas the constructive trust is *"identifying the true beneficial owner or owners, and the size of their beneficial interest"*;[43] the cure to a proprietary estoppel claim can be anything the court sees fit to right the wrong, including a monetary award as in *Habberfield v Habberfield*[44] when the youngest daughter was promised a stake in the farm's dairy unit by her father. However, upon his death he left the farm to his widow who then closed down the dairy unit. The Court of Appeal deemed a £1.17million award by the High Court suitable to make amends for her father's going back on his promise. A constructive trust could (presumably) potentially have been an option of the court but various factors pointed towards the compensation.

This 'common-intention' constructive trust is therefore merely another tool in the equity court's armoury. One might argue, like Waters, that a common-intention constructive trust is not a freestanding type of trust but merely a tool or remedy to rectify a breach of equity law as much as common or statutory law; the common-intention is merely an inherent ingredient of the equitable principles which a constructive trust may, or may not, be employed to enforce.

Resulting and constructive trusts each have variants, all overlapping to some degree within themselves; but resulting and constructive trust also overlap with each other to some extent. Whatever the title, they both remove the beneficial ownership away from the legal title, they go against the official transaction - the one recognised by common law. They use equitable principles to ensure that the common law position cannot stand; either because of the what the parties must have wanted (but did not do), or because the law of equity and good conscience itself wants it to happen. The title of the trusts just changes with the circumstances within which the trusts are employed.

---

[41] [2000] Ch 162

[42] [2007] 2 AC 432 (HL) at 448

[43] Ibid at 448

[44] [2019] EWCA Civ 890

IMPLIED TRUSTS

3 What is modern tax law?

"The Common Law of England has been laboriously built about a mythical figure – the figure of 'The Reasonable Man'" [1]

Before looking at how implied trusts and beneficial ownership made their way into modern tax law, it is worth looking at what the latter term means. I will take 'modern tax law' to mean those rules which emanate from, and are interpreted and enforced by, the three branches of state according to the doctrine of separation of powers:[2] the Judiciary, Parliament and the Executive; represented by the tax tribunals and courts, tax legislation and HMRC respectively.

3.1 Tax Tribunals – The Judiciary

Until 1 April 2009, the tax court of first instance was that of the General Commissioners (who were unpaid and, until 1958, required to own property). The General Commissioners were made up of laymen to hear appeals concerning Inland Revenue (IR) and later, HMRC assessments. Appeals from there went to the Special Commissioners, a body formed of professional judges. Before its abolition in 1880, tax disputes had gone to the Court of Exchequer; after that date they went to the Chancery Division of the High Court.

Following the 2009 reforms, the professional Special Commissioners were transferred to the Tax Chamber (one of eleven such chambers) of the First Tier Tribunal (FTT), the new court of first instance and thus effective replacement of the old lay General Commissioners. The Tax & Chancery Chamber (one of four such chambers) of the Upper Tribunal (UT) acts as the appeal court from the FTT and consists of some of the old Special Commissioners as well as judges from the Chancery Division of the High Court. From the UT, appeals now go straight to the civil division of the Court of Appeal (or Court of Sessions in Scotland). The UT, as a senior Court of Record, has equivalent status to the High Court and now fulfils the role of the Chancery Division in tax matters; the name, 'Tax & Chancery Chamber' points to the connection.

This effective merging of the Special Commissioners into the Chancery Division of the High Court coincides nicely with considerations about how implied trusts found their way into the tax courts. Arguably, the tax courts

---

[1]A. P. Herbert (1890-1971), *'Uncommon Law'* (1935)

[2]Loosely using De Montesquieu's 'distribution of powers' principle in *"Spirit of the Laws"* (1748)

found their way into the chancery courts, bringing a largely administrative tribunal system into the well of a court which had been harbouring and nurturing equitable principles and trusts for centuries. And, just as a fitting finish, the Chancery Court, in its modern incarnation as a division, is now headed by a Chancellor once again.

There is more detail below about the journey from the old medieval equity courts to today's senior courts.

3.2   Legislation – Parliament

Statute is the principal source of tax law and there were several income tax Acts before the imposition of a permanent income tax Act in 1842. There have also been regular 'Tax Acts' passed by Parliament, and several cases discussed below concern the Income Tax Act 1952. The Labour government under Tony Blair in 1997 oversaw an explosion in legislation; until then the Income & Corporation Taxes Act (ICTA) 1988 alone had contained the relevant legislation for income tax. The Income Tax (Earnings & Pension) Act (ITEPA) 2003, the Income Tax (Trading & Other Income) Act (ITTOIA) 2005 and ITA 2007 now contain the modern legislation for income tax. The Capital Gains Tax (CGT) legislation is contained within the Taxation of Chargeable Gains Act (TCGA) 1992, with that for Inheritance Tax (IHT) contained within the Inheritance Tax Act (IHTA) 1984.

3.3   HMRC – The Executive

His Majesty's Revenue & Customs, a non-ministerial department of the UK government, was created on 18 April 2005 following the passing of the Commissioners for Revenue & Customs Act 2005. This Act merged the old IR (responsible for the collection of direct taxes, National Insurance and stamp taxes) with Her Majesty's Customs & Excise (responsible for VAT, as well as customs and excise duties).

The onset of the Anglo-Dutch wars and resulting need for funds, combined with the accumulation of numerous, haphazard indirect taxes imposed over the centuries (on things such as ships, hearths, windows and even servants), led to the creation of the Board of Taxes in 1665. This became the Board of Stamps and Taxes in 1833 and finally the Board of the Inland Revenue in 1848 manned by its commissioners.

HMRC is the odd one out in the trilogy of tax law as it is not a law-making institution; it is a functionary, assessing and collecting taxes on behalf of the Crown. But within a constitutional monarchy this means it is essentially an arm of the executive, with the work being carried out by civil servants within a government department. Ordinarily, it would not come under any heading relating to tax law, but in examining the status of beneficial interest through implied trusts in today's tax law, it would seem wise to look at the position that HMRC takes on the matter. Thankfully, HMRC make available their own guidance manuals, which give an insight to their attitude and approach towards, and interpretation of, the tax cases and legislation. Whilst HMRC's opinions are neither binding (nor arguably of any great academic interest), they are essentially the voice of the executive and as such their views certainly are valuable from a practical perspective and give another angle when reviewing the position of beneficial ownership and implied trusts within tax law.

4 How does the law distinguish between implied trusts and express trusts?

"At all events, Chancery will work none of its bad influences on us. We have happily been brought together, thanks to our good kinsman, and it can't divide us now!"[1]

Having looked at what an implied trust is, it is worth looking at the other end of the spectrum toward express trusts and what role they play in the role of beneficial ownership in tax.

As mentioned above, an express trust is one whereby the terms are 'expressly', intentionally or deliberately stated in a deed or a deceased's will. Expressly spoken words may suffice, but as a basic requirement equity demands proof that is has been created[2] and from 1677, for any trust involving land, proof in writing was required. Sometimes, an express trust can be created by the written word, but not in the way the 'settlor' meant. A good example of this is the case of *Vincent*.[3] In that case, a will with a clause in it which allowed a man to continue living in the house for the rest of his life was construed as an 'Interest in Possession' (IIP) or 'life interest' trust which gave him a right to benefit from the asset for the rest of his life. So even an express trust can have its terms implied as far as interpretation of the deed or will is concerned.

It is possible for an express trust to be formed verbally, as alluded to in *Cook v. Fountain* above. The case of *Paul v. Constance*[4] was reviewed by the Court of Appeal where it was held that, by repeatedly saying "the money is as much yours as mine" in respect of a bank account, an express trust had been created. The court held that a trustee need not necessarily state categorically that he is a trustee, or indeed that a trust exists at all; but it was held in that case that there was sufficient evidence of the trust's existence. However, the Court of Appeal only held that an express trust was in place because no argument had been made about the creation of an implied trust, which would be based upon the parties' presumed intention:

"...one must exclude from one's mind any case built upon the existence of an implied or constructive trust, for this case was put forward at the trial and is

---

[1] Charles Dickens, *Bleak House*, chapter 5

[2] *Mynn v. Cobb* (1604) Cary 25; *Spring v. Upton* (1579) Cary 81

[3] TC7432 October 2019 (FTT)

[4] [1977] 1 WLR 527

now argued by the plaintiff as one of express declaration of trust. It was so pleaded and it is only as such that it may be considered in this court. The question, therefore, is whether, in all the circumstances, the use of those words on numerous occasions as between the deceased and the plaintiff constituted an express declaration of trust".[5]

Had the option of an implied trusts been available to the court, then it is likely that an implied trust would have been imposed to give the plaintiff a beneficial interest in the bank account, as the High Court did in *Young v. Sealey.*[6] Whilst the effective result would have been the same either way, the trust would likely have been implied by the court on the basis of the verbal assurances given, rather than as an express trust with nothing in writing. Intentions are certainly easier to prove if they are written down, something perhaps in the mind of Lord Nottingham when the Statute of Frauds was being drafted in 1677.

Whilst both express and implied trusts are united in having a split of legal and beneficial ownership, their tax treatment is very different.

4.1   Express trusts

With express trusts, the trustees are accountable for all income tax, CGT and (usually) IHT liabilities of the trust and pay taxes at their own rates; indeed, different types of trust pay income taxes at different rates: IIP trusts at basic rate, with discretionary trusts at additional rate. Discretionary and many IIP trusts are also subject to their own IHT ('relevant property') regime with 10-yearly and exit charges.

Trustees are given their own Unique Tax Reference Number by HMRC and complete their own trust income tax/CGT returns (SA900); there is no immediate onus on the beneficiaries at all to account for the income tax stemming from the assets of which they have use, unless income is mandated directly to them.

The point is that the onus of all income tax, CGT and IHT liability falls upon the legal owners – the trustees. The fact that beneficial ownership lies with someone else is ignored for tax purposes as far as express trusts are concerned.

---

[5] Per Scarman LJ at 532

[6][1949] 1 All ER 92 (Ch D)

4.2   Implied trusts

With implied trusts there is no such systematic method for tax assessment on the trustees. The trustees are almost incidental and a necessity purely for establishing the beneficial ownership elsewhere. Indeed, implied trustees can have trusteeship imposed upon them unknowingly, even unwillingly. If beneficial ownership has been bestowed upon beneficiaries under an implied trust, they are deemed to own it absolutely – there is no formal trust mechanism above them as there is with an express trust whereby the trustees are assessable for the tax. Therefore, someone who is deemed to own the beneficial title of an asset is subject to income tax, CGT and IHT as if they owned the asset absolutely, even though the legal title lies elsewhere. This is how bare trusts are taxed – they are transparent for tax purposes.[7]

Implied trusts are therefore, in many respects, something of a misnomer for the simple reason that HMRC does not actually treat them as express trusts and separate tax entities. 'Implied beneficial ownership' rather than 'implied trust' would be a more accurate description as far as the tax treatment is concerned; but because UK courts would not order the seizure of the legal title of an asset off one person and give it to another, all they can do is pass the beneficial ownership to that other person using their equitable jurisdiction either because there's been a breach of common law, equity or on the basis of presumed intentions. However, as the legal and beneficial titles have been split, the term 'trust' is attached to the arrangement, but that is the only thing in common with an express trust.

The whole basis of an implied trust is the result of the interpretation of the courts, legislation and HMRC as to the rightful ownership of an asset in a manner they see as equitable and to henceforth regard the beneficiary as the absolute owner of that asset; therefore, they are taxed accordingly. Whereas if the trust has been expressly established in line with the parties' express wishes, then HMRC can treat it as a separate (tax) entity and tax the trustees as owners by trust tax rates.

Therefore, as far as tax is concerned, an implied trust is essentially a bare trust, with the beneficiary being treated as the absolute owner. Bare trusts are effectively the tax law's translation of implied trusts. It is not HMRC's concern, nor that of the UK tax law generally, how the beneficial ownership came to be split – the words 'implied', 'resulting' or 'constructive' are pretty much immaterial to them, which is probably why we see so little of them in

---

[7]HMRC Guidance TSEM1563

legislation, cases and guidance. HMRC just need to know whether to tax the trustee of an express trust, or the beneficiary of a bare trust.

Whilst a bare trust is usually constituted in writing, they can be created verbally like express trusts; the difference with an express trust though is that the tax burden will fall elsewhere than it would with bare/implied trusts. In the case of *Tang v. HMRC*,[8] verbal statements by the appellant's parents-in-law that money in her bank account was beneficially owned by them, along with the fact that the appellant did not withdraw any funds, were all sufficient evidence that a bare trust existed; it was an implied trust, and it was a bare trust. It is similar to the case of *Aroso v. Coutts*[9] whereby beneficial ownership was recognised through an implied trust. However, in *Aroso* this was centred around a gifting of the capital and was thus classified as a resulting trust; whereas *Tang* was merely looking at the status of the bank account. Either way, the end result was the same – beneficial ownership was implied by the tax court's equitable jurisdiction in the absence of writing and using conduct as evidence.

Partnerships are arguably a form of bare trust too as far as tax law is concerned.

4.3   Partnerships

A partnership, whether it be an ordinary partnership, a limited partnership or a limited liability partnership (an LLP – which is a separate legal entity throughout the UK), is transparent for tax purposes. This means the partners own their respective shares in the underlying partnership assets and are taxed accordingly for income tax and CGT on their own income/capital gain allocation. Even in Scotland, where the ordinary partnership is a 'firm' for legal purposes with partners owning their share of that firm rather than just the underlying assets, it is treated the same as English partnerships for tax purposes. Thus, there is UK consensus on the tax treatment of partnerships.

But what have partnerships got to do with trusts and beneficial ownership?

In many respects a partnership is a lot like a bare trust in that the legal and beneficial ownership may lie with different people. Land is indeed held in

---

[8](2019) UKUT 0081

[9][2002] 1 All ER 241 (Ch D)

trust by the legal owners.[10]There has been some question whether the same can be said for other assets. Partnership Act 1890 s.20(1) states:

> *"All property and rights and interests in property originally brought into the partnership stock or acquired, whether by purchase or otherwise, on account of the firm, or for the purposes and in the course of the partnership business, are called in this Act partnership property, and must be <u>held and applied</u> by the partners exclusively for the purposes of the partnership and in accordance with the partnership agreement".*

Unlike with s.20(2), the word 'trust' is not mentioned anywhere; the underlined part would tend to indicate an agency relationship[11] rather than one of trusteeship.

Certain partners may be the legal owners of the partnership assets but with the beneficial ownership lying with all the partners. As far as income tax, IHT and CGT are concerned, the revenue and capital profits and losses are therefore assessed upon the beneficial owners (i.e. the partners) rather than just the legal owners. The law of trust and that of agency are different, but when the same person is a legal owner, being an agent is effectively akin to being a nominee which is, in turn, akin to bare trusteeship. The laws of agency and trust are different and so a distinction is perfectly viable if the legislation says a trust is expressed in one sub-section, but not in another. HMRC's guidance would also point toward the partnership as a whole being more akin to a trust due to the fact that a partner's profit share need not have any correspondence with capital or effort contributed.[12] *Lindley & Banks* says much the same thing in relation to capital profits ratio and the actual share in the asset:

> *"The fact that the capital profits attributable to a particular asset e.g. goodwill, are to be shared by the partners in equal shares does not necessarily mean that it is partnership property in which all the partners are interested in the same shares"* [13]

---

[10]Per Partnership Act 1890 s.20(2) which states that land *"which belongs to the partnership shall devolve according to the nature and tenure thereof, and general rules thereto applicable, <u>but in trust, so far as necessary, for the persons beneficially interested in the land</u> under this section"*

[11]Discussed and questioned in "Lindley & Banks on Partnership" section 18-06 where the case of *Horler v. Rubin* [2011] BPIR 718 discussed the matter and the judge, HHJ Raynor QC said it was an agency and not a trustee holding. Whilst the case was overturned on appeal, that point was not mentioned again.

[12]HMRC Guidance PM137000

[13]*"Lindley & Banks on Partnership"* section 18-06

IMPLIED TRUSTS

Lindley & Banks also (arguably) hints at the idea of a partnership being an implied trust focusing on the common or presumed intentions of the parties. When looking at whether a partner has contributed property to the partnership in the absence of any express partnership agreement, it says:

> *"The court will not, however, find an implied agreement to bring assets in as partnership property where that would not accord with the subjective intentions of the partners, irrespective of any objective appearances".*[14]

This would accord with the view that a partnership is essentially a trust. Partnerships are usually governed by a written agreement, but the underlying intentions of the partners will ultimately determine the partnership's governance. However, a partnership agreement is merely the written record of those intentions, rather than a deed of trust. The absence of an agreement will cause the Partnership Act 1890 to impose basic statutory intentions, and the principles of equity will impose an implied trust over the partnership assets in any event, but under potentially unfavourable terms.

---

[14]Ibid in section 18-06

5 When did beneficial ownership become the focus of income tax legislation?

"And it came to pass in those days, that there went out a decree from Caesar Augustus, that all the world should be taxed"[1]

Having examined the mechanisms of implied trusts, it is time to examine the most valuable and everyday tax to which these trusts are subject: income tax.

The imposition of beneficial ownership via implied trusts affects all taxes, but CGT and IHT are only relevant for transactions and/or death, whereas income tax affects far more people and far more often; every year it brings far more revenue into the Exchequer than any capital tax. Income tax yielded £195billion in 2019/20 and accounted for over 23% of total revenue receipts, compared to only £31billion for the capital taxes.[2] Just as in the last century, ensuring that people pay the correct amount of tax on their income is clearly an important duty of the government, and countering the artificial assignment of beneficial ownership is therefore paramount.

The first income tax Act was brought into force by Pitt the Younger in 1799 to fund the Napoleonic wars at a rate of 2d in the £ for incomes over £60. It remained in place until 1802 when the Peace of Amiens led to its abolition. However, it was reintroduced a year later and brought in the principle of taxation at source, as well as introducing the Schedules of income, most of which survived until 2005 (although Schedules A and D still survive for corporation tax). The 1806 Act declared that married couples would have their joint income taxed as one by the husband; prior to this, the wife's own income was not even acknowledged. Further similar Acts were introduced until 1816 when the tax was placed in abeyance. Income tax would finally become a permanent feature in 1842 under Robert Peel.

But when did beneficial ownership become a concern of income tax? The acts of avoidance which led to its introduction a hundred years ago exploited the fact that income tax only focused on the legal ownership of income sources and its associated deductions; the settlements legislation took root within income tax legislation in 1922. The legislation for TOAA goes back even further, appearing in an early form within the 1842 Act, though not being clearly defined and appearing in its modern form until the 1936 Act. This

---

[1] St Luke. Ch. 2, v. 1

[2] According to "Tax Statistics - House of Commons briefing paper" (CBP-8513 September 2020. Matthew Keep)

will be examined in more detail below. These pieces of legislation identified a true beneficial owner of income and effectively imposed an implied trust to enforce the beneficial ownership to ensure the 'real' owner remained liable for income tax. So beneficial ownership has arguably been recognised by the legislation since income tax's permanent inception, albeit not properly defined until the early 20th century.

However, who is actually chargeable on earned income within the income tax Acts?

The 1842 Act defined "persons chargeable under the Act" as:

> *"All persons receiving income in their own right, trustees and guardians of incapacitated persons......agents and factors"*

The 1952 Taxes Act defined the same, under the various Schedules as:

> *"the occupier"* who is *"any person having the use of any lands and tenements"* for Schedule A (s.105);
> *"the person entitled to the profits, dividends or proceeds"* for Schedule C (s.118); and
> *"person receiving or entitled to receive the income"* for Schedule D (s.148).

There is only one type of income subject to beneficial, as opposed to legal, entitlement that is specifically mentioned, and that is 'surtax' – the super tax for higher earners introduced in 1909 which lasted until 1973 when it was replaced with a higher rate band for income tax. Section 234(2) of the 1952 Act makes reference to intermediaries who are required to furnish information to HMRC's predecessor, the IR, of those:

> *"beneficially entitled to the income in question"*

Other than this reference, the tax burden therefore falls on the legal owner of the source of income. The reference to persons *"receiving"* or being *"entitled to receive"* income is mentioned throughout the legislation right up to the modern pieces of legislation. The ICTA 1970 and 1988 only made reference to beneficial ownership of shares for income tax purposes (outside the settlements and TOAA chapters); it was not until the Income Taxes Act (ITA) 2007 that explicit mentions of beneficial ownership started to permeate the other income tax laws such as property ownership (s.836), royalty payments (s.911) and gifting shares and property to charity (s.431).

Beneficial ownership, whilst mentioned within various parts of the income tax legislation, is recognised predominantly through the courts – indeed it is the courts which impose the implied trusts and who recognise the real entitled owner of the income, often in defiance of the legislation. HMRC form their own interpretation of ownership, taking the legislation which has been tempered by years of court precedents.

But first we should look at one of the core pieces of income tax legislation of which implied trusts are central: the settlements legislation.

6   What is the settlements legislation? And how does it fit in with implied trusts and income tax law?

"I wrote to you some time ago about the income tax wishing to know what way ours could be given in to be the least burdensome. Persons under sixty pounds a year, I understand, pay nothing, could we not take advantage of this in some way?"[1]

Having looked at the status of beneficial ownership within income tax legislation, it is clear that such ownership has only been consistently (throughout the 20th century) and expressly outlined within that focused on settlements and TOAA chapters, both of which are anti-avoidance provisions. It is only recently that it has been widely used within the rest of the legislation.

The settlements legislation was first introduced by the Finance Act 1922 but subject to slightly harsher changes through the following decades (Finance Acts 1936, 1938 and 1948; Income Tax Act 1952 and ICTA 1970 and 1988). The modern legislation is now to be found in ITTOIA 2005 ss 624-648.

The settlements legislation is the ultimate example of implied trusts being exhibited within the taxation legislation and courts. A settlement is a trust; it is being implied and subsequently imposed by the legislation and thus recognised and enforced by the courts. The person who created the settlement is the settlor; if the person who benefits is the settlor, their spouse or minor unmarried child, then the settlor is taxed upon those beneficiaries' income.

The definition of a 'settlement' is, and always has been, very wide. The word itself first appeared in the Finance Act 1936 and was defined as:

"the expression 'disposition' includes any trust, covenant, agreement or arrangement"[2]

ITTOIA 2005 s.620(1) now defines it as:

"any disposition, trust, covenant, agreement, arrangement or transfer of assets (except that it does not include a charitable loan arrangement)"

---

[1]William Wordsworth, in a letter to his Attorney brother Richard, December 1805

[2]Section 21(9)b)

Thus, little has changed as far as the definition of a settlement is concerned; indeed, as Lord Walker stated in the *Jones v. Garnett* (aka *'Arctic Systems'*) case:

"it has a long and fairly complicated pedigree"[3]

Put simply, the settlements legislation will impose a settlor-interested trust in place of the offending 'settlement'. The settlors will therefore be taxed as if that income diverted through the settlement was actually theirs because they failed to properly gift it. Because of the very wide definition of settlement, essentially anything which causes income to be diverted to someone else under a 'bounteous' or un-commercial 'arrangement' (or simply one not at arm's length) resulting in a lower income tax charge as would otherwise arise, could fall foul of the legislation. This 'bounty' criterion was first highlighted by Plowman J in *IRC v. Leiner*[4]. If the beneficiary concerned is the settlor's spouse/civil partner, the income diverted to the spouse must be *"wholly or substantially a right to income"*[5] to come within the legislation. Outright gifts (those of income with some corresponding capital rights etc behind them) between spouses fall within an exemption.

In HMRC's eyes the settlor is the real source of the income and so the settlements legislation recognises him as the rightful payer of the tax. The settlor is defined in ITTOIA 2005 s.620 (1) as:

"any person by whom the settlement was made"

Section 620(3) expands on this explaining that a settlor is a person who:

"(a) has provided funds directly or indirectly for the purpose of the settlement,
(b) has undertaken to provide funds directly or indirectly for the purpose of the settlement, or
(c) has made a reciprocal arrangement with another person for the other person to make or enter into the settlement"

The provision above allows for the legislation to be applied when a settlor provides funds even indirectly, thus widening the potential scenarios coming within the settlements legislation even further. Examples would include: dividend waivers (resulting in such dividends ending up in the

---

[3][2007] 1 WLR 2030 at 2041

[4](1964) 41 TC 589 at 596

[5]Section 626 – the spousal exemption, which I shall be discussing separately below

IMPLIED TRUSTS

hands of shareholders paying tax at a lower rate) and even partnerships where a partner receives more profit than their capital share warrants. Also, the settlor would be the person whose labour is the source of the funds - several such cases will be reviewed below.

Within the legislation and cases, little mention is made of the word 'trusts', let alone 'implied trusts'; nor is there any reference to equitable principles. It is a straightforward anti-avoidance provision, but it belongs in this book because it is effectively an implied trust. A gift has been made, but the donor is still able to benefit as if they'd never given it; the legal ownership has been transferred as part of the settlement. As a result of this, the express arrangement is reclassified as an implied settlor-interested trust, whereby the donor is treated as a beneficial owner. This implied settlor-interested trust could be a constructive trust in the sense that, as far as HMRC is concerned, they are being used to right a moral (if not a legal) wrong. It could be a common intention resulting trust, it being intended by the parties for the donor and their family to benefit from it. It could also be an automatic resulting trust, a failure by the donor to fully divest themselves of an income-producing asset and so the express settlement fails. Whatever the precise classification, this legislation, like that for transfer of assets overseas, is a statutory imposition of a non-descript implied trust.

6.1 Why was it necessary to introduce the settlements legislation?

The reason was as relevant in the early twentieth (and even nineteenth) century as it is today: people were diverting their income onto others and thus shifting the income tax liability onto those others.

At the time, the issue was not so much with husbands' diverting income to their wives; until 1990 a wife's income was taxed as her husband's anyway. The issue was income being diverted to other family members. Things got a little harder in 1803 when Addington's income tax legislation became based on the principle of taxation at source and the use of settlements became more prevalent than simple deductions. Bringing one's own income down to below Pitt's original £60 threshold (c.£5,140 in today's money) would take one out of the income tax regime altogether. This tax-free 'allowance' was reduced to £50 in 1806 but raised to £150 (c.£17,000 today) when income tax became a permanent feature in 1842. Despite the historical equivalent of the personal allowance being so high, granting an annuity to one's children to avoid the income tax was becoming widespread by the mid-1800s according to David Stopforth.[6] In the same article, Stopforth gives a selection of exchanges within the Select Committee on income and Property Tax in the summer of 1851; one of the commissioners gave this as an example of what was going on:

> "... a farmer who is the owner and occupier of a farm at £140 per annum ... would be assessed at £4/1/8d under Schedule A for the value and at £2/-/10d for the occupation, under Schedule D. His son, ... was employed upon the farm; he ostensibly makes the son his tenant, by which means the father can claim the £140 for the value of the farm, and the son can claim under Schedule D as the occupier at £140. The exemption runs up to £300 a year ... I believe that was done in Derbyshire to a great extent, and in other parts of the country, after the first year. This is what I would describe perhaps as a legal avoidance; it is not a fraud; it is merely the management."

However, little was done to legislate against the use of settlements; not until the case of CIR v. Wilson[7] in 1927 did the IR seem keen to even pursue such matters. In that case, the House of Lords held that a father who had purchased shares in his 10-year-old son's name had effectively made a gift to his son.

Following the First World War and the introduction of the 'super-tax', the use of avoidance settlements was increasing and thus depriving the Treasury of even greater sums. A Royal Commission on Income tax had been formed in 1920 and had identified the widespread use of legal avoidance methods and recommended their closure. The resulting Finance Act 1922 targeted revocable and short-term disposition of income and annual covenants which had been deductible income, but it did not affect dispositions of property, so its effect was limited.

A further Royal Commission (The 'Colwyn Committee'[8]) was convened in 1928 to review how to remedy the situation. A further example of post-war settlements use was given by Mr E R Harrison (Assistant Secretary to the Board of IR):

> "A had originally an income of £15,000 a year. The amount of super-tax payable for 1918/19 on an income of £15,000 would be £2,312. If A has alienated or charged this income so that only £3,000 now remains to him

---

[6]"Settlement and the avoidance of tax on income – period to 1920" (BTR 1990, 7, 225)

[7](1927) 13 TC 789

[8]The Colwyn Committee and the Incidence of Income Tax, 1928

whilst £2,000 represents the income of each of his six children A will pay only £62 in super-tax and his children will be totally exempt"

It was not until the Finance Act 1936 that income within revocable settlements on minor children became taxable upon the settlor; the Finance Act 1938 clamped down on lending the settlor's annual payments back to him as well as irrevocable settlements. It is in these two Acts in particular that we see the foundations for the modern legislation.

The current legislation allows for three scenarios:
1. the settlement is one in which the settlor retains an interest as a beneficiary (i.e. a pure settlor-interested trust) (s.624);
2. when the minor, unmarried children of that settlor are beneficiaries (s.629); or
3. when capital sums are paid by the trustees to the settlor (s.633) (or by a corporate body connected to the settlement, s.641). This 'capital sum' scenarios can apply even when the trustees are repaying a commercial-rate loan.

Sections 624 and 629 are often considered together as settlements legislation and are frequently an issue when a settlor has diverted income to his family members including minors. The 'capital sum' scenarios are not discussed here; the focus is on those whereby the trust is implied by the court because an arrangement whereby the income is gifted to someone else is deemed to be a 'settlement'. In most 'capital sum' scenarios the formal (express) trust is already in place and is one from which the settlor has been able to benefit.

6.2   Settlor or their children retains an interest

One point to make about a settlor-interested trust whereby the donor's minor, unmarried children can benefit, is that for income tax purposes there is a de minimis. Where the income coming from the settled asset is £100 or less, then the child beneficiary will indeed be taxed under their own name, just as the settlement intended. Beyond that, the settlements legislation will take effect.

This is the main type of implied trust which IR and HMRC have been seeking (and often succeeding) to impose for many years. As mentioned above, due to the very wide definition of a 'settlement' and the possibility of indirect gifting by the donor being sufficient to trigger the legislation, there are numerous scenarios which could come under the settlements legislation. Indeed, some scenarios may have nothing to do with actual express trusts being re-categorised as settlor-interested. There are some scenarios within HMRC's guidance which are headed 'non-trust' but would still be deemed as coming within the remit of the legislation.

6.2.1 Partnerships – HMRC guidance

Essentially, partnerships are treated in exactly the same way as any 'arrangement' within the definition of a settlement. After all, as we have established, a partnership is effectively a type of bare trust. Whilst partners' profits do not have to match their capital contribution, if the mismatch is such that it would be deemed to be bounteous to themselves or their spouses/minor children, then the settlements legislation might apply:

> "Where the incoming partner receives a share of profits out of all proportion to the contribution made to the partnership, the arrangement would include an element of bounty".[9]

HMRC give some examples of when the settlements legislation may or may not apply in a partnership scenario and use that of a sleeping partner. By doing this they are focusing on the actual capital investment of a partner, rather than any personal skills or qualifications they may be introducing, which may be the case with professional (rather than trading) partnerships. One such example is where the legislation would not apply is:

> "Mr and Mrs O and their friend Mr P have a business idea. They want to open a Cycle Repair Shop. Mrs O does not want to work but agrees to invest in the business without taking an active part, that is to say she is a sleeping partner. Each partner invests £10,000 and the £30,000 is used to lease a shop, buy equipment and stock and keep the business going until trade builds up. Under the partnership agreement Mr O and Mr P receive £500 a week with all the remaining profits split three ways between the partners.

> The business is a huge success and makes large profits and continues to grow. Within five years Mrs O is receiving £50,000 a year as her share of the partnership profits. Although Mrs O does not work in the business, and her initial investment has turned out to be very successful, the settlements legislation would not apply to treat her share of the partnership profits as Mr O's. Mrs O's original investment was vital to get the business started and she risked losing it if the business failed".[10]

At this stage, the fact that the sleeping partner is a spouse of another partner is irrelevant as Mrs O has contributed capital and so there is no question of her only receiving a gift of income from a settlor. The question here is whether her profits are a proportionate return on her investment and whether there is commercial justification behind it. Here, HMRC's view is

---

[9]HMRC Guidance TSEM4215
[10]Ibid

that an investing partner is receiving a proportionate reward for the risk of investing in a start-up business. Were any third-party investors to take such a risk and help a start-up, they would undoubtedly expect a return reflecting that risk. This is to be contrasted with another example in the same piece of guidance:

"Mr Y, an architect, commences business as a sole trader. The business is successful and a few years later annual profits are in the region of £80,000. The business is transferred to a new partnership of Mr & Mrs Y. A deed is executed under which income profits are to be shared equally but the rights to share in capital profits belong solely to Mr Y. Mrs Y subscribes no new capital and carries out no work whatsoever for the partnership, that is to say she is a sleeping partner. Profits for the year are £80,000 and £40,000 belongs to Mrs Y. This is a bounteous arrangement transferring income from one spouse to another. The settlements legislation will apply and Mrs Y's share of the profits will continue to be assessed on Mr Y.

Where the incoming partner is not a spouse or civil partner the legislation will not apply unless there are arrangements or conditions where the property can revert to the settlor (or spouse or civil partner)".

This example is focusing on spousal exemption and thus on whether or not Mrs Y has been made a gift of pure income. As she has contributed no capital or personal input, her profit share would be deemed as bounteous and thus taxed upon Mr Y who is generating the profit.

That final paragraph does make express reference to a settlor-interested trust and the simple causative scenario which would bring this about, with the settlor being entitled to the underlying property. However, this is a useful reminder of what a basic settlor-interested trust is and that a partnership is effectively a form of trust.

HMRC's guidance, as we have seen above, gives a useful insight into their approach and interpretation of legislation. They have given some guidance about 'non-trust' scenarios and factors which may attract their attention; clearly, they are looking to impose a settlor-interested trust into non-trust situations such as:

i.   *"Disproportionately large returns on capital investments.*

ii.   *Differing classes of shares enabling dividends to be paid only to shareholders paying lower rates of tax.*

iii.   *Dividends being waived so that higher dividends can be paid to shareholders paying lower rates of tax.*

iv.   *Income being transferred from the person making most of the profits of a business to a friend or family member who pays tax at a lower rate[11]".*

The second of HMRC's examples is the alphabet shares; the third being dividend waivers. The fourth is the general non-trust scenario, which, in most instances would likely be a partnership. Oddly, this last point[12] makes reference to 'friends' (however they might be defined), beyond the legislative scope of settlor, their spouse and minor children. This might give some insight into the desired scope of HMRC's application of the legislation if they can argue that the settlor, their spouse/children could benefit, however indirectly, from an uncommercial arrangement with a 'friend'.

6.2.2   Dividend waivers – HMRC guidance

Prior to a limited company's declaring a dividend for a unitary class of shares, an individual shareholder has every right not to receive it and be treated accordingly; having done this, for both legal and tax purposes the shareholder has not received the dividend. The profits that would have been received by that shareholder return to the company's distributable profits. On that face of it, at this stage, there is no reason why HMRC would have any interest in such an innocuous arrangement. However, those waived profits going back into the company's reserves will eventually make their way to other shareholders, thus facilitating gifts of income in the form of those foregone dividends and thus potentially attracting the wrath of the settlements legislation.

HMRC's guidance makes clear that not all dividend waivers will attract the settlements legislation. However, were it to be taken to greater lengths than HMRC deem to be commercial, then the legislation may apply. The same guidance[13] gives the public examples of scenarios and surrounding situations which, in their view, would attract the legislation:

"The level of retained profits, including the retained profits of subsidiary companies, is insufficient to allow the same rate of dividend to be paid on all issued share capital.

Although there are sufficient retained profits to pay the same rate of dividend per share for the year in question, there has been a succession of waivers over

---

[11] TSEM4325

[12] Along with guidance in TSEM4320 stating: *"Most commonly the legislation will apply where individuals seek to divert income to members of their family or to friends"*

[13] HMRC Guidance TSEM4225

several years where the total dividends payable in the absence of the waivers exceed accumulated realised profits.

There is any other evidence, which suggests that the same rate would not have been paid on all the issued shares in the absence of the waiver.

The non-waiving shareholders are persons whom the waiving shareholder can reasonably be regarded as wishing to benefit by the waiver.

The non-waiving shareholder would pay less tax on the dividend than the waiving shareholder".

In the same guidance, HMRC give the following example of a scenario in which they might apply the legislation:

"Mrs H owns 80 ordinary shares in H Limited. Mr H owns 20 shares. In 2000, the company made a profit of £25,000. Mrs H waived her right to any dividend. The company then declared a dividend of £1,000 per share, and Mr H, who had no other income, received a dividend of £20,000.

No property has been transferred so the settlement is one of income. As such, the exemption for outright gifts to spouses is not in point and we would apply the settlements legislation in these circumstances. Clearly a dividend of this amount could not have been paid from the company's profits on all the shares, so the waiver arrangement enhanced the dividend paid to Mr H. £16,000 of the dividend paid to Mr H is attributed to Mrs H under ITTOIA/S624 because the waiver was a bounteous arrangement".

As a potential pure gift of income, the spousal exemption would not apply and so they are susceptible to the legislation just as a non-married couple. The only question concerns commerciality and whether the capital held warrants the amount of income.

6.2.3   Alphabet shares – HMRC guidance

Alphabet shares are on the same lines as dividend waivers: disproportionate dividend payments in relation to the underlying shareholding. Usually, the shares are still ordinary shares and pari passu, but merely a different class just to allow different rates of dividends to be declared. This may be to preserve distributable reserves within the company for any number of commercial reasons. But, if all shareholders receive the same amount per share, the majority shareholders would suffer a larger tax burden. By waiving those dividends, they are saving themselves from that higher tax burden. However, this is tax avoidance as far as HMRC is concerned, hence the settlements legislation.

In practice, when varying levels of dividend per share are to be paid to the shareholders for whatever reason, alphabet shares are the simplest way to facilitate that process; declaring A and B share dividends at different rates is generally easier than administering dividend waivers. From an accountants' perspective, there is a regulatory aspect which makes declaring dividends at a different rate more favourable than declaring waivers. As a waiver of a dividend involves no consideration from the shareholder, it is not a valid contract; in order for it to be valid it needs to be in the form of a deed, the execution of which is a reserved legal activity[14]. Currently solicitors and barristers are authorised to execute deeds, whereas members of the professional bodies for chartered accountants are not.

In the same guidance as above for the dividend waivers, HMRC give an example of when alphabet shares might also trigger the legislation – expanding upon the dividend wavier scenario:

> "… Mrs I owns A shares and Mr I owns B shares. Both A and B shares rank equally. Again profits of £25,000 are made and a dividend of £20,000 is voted on the B shares while no dividend is voted on the A shares.
>
> Clearly by not voting dividends on the A shares (which rank equally with the B shares) this is a bounteous arrangement as the dividend paid on the B shares could only be paid if no dividend was declared in respect of the A shares. £16,000 of the dividend paid to Mr I is attributed to Mrs I under ITTOIA/S624 because the decision only to vote dividends on certain shares was a bounteous arrangement".

Clearly therefore, alphabet shares and dividend waivers are different sides of the same coin – certainly as far as HMRC are concerned. They both facilitate dividends' being diverted to a shareholder whose underlying shares do not warrant such a payment. They are both imposing settlor-interested implied trusts on the recipient shareholder in favour of the settlor to whom, in HMRC's view, they actually belong.

6.2.4   Cases

As with the guidance, cases are a useful illustration of when IR and HMRC have sought to impose the settlements legislation; but each case will probably be unique on its facts and thus of little use as a precedent. There have a great number of settlements legislation cases throughout the last century and we shall look into three well-known ones to illustrate when IR (as they were in all these cases) sought to impose these implied trusts. One

---

[14] Under Legal Services Act 2007 Schedule 2

was heard before the High Court, one before the Court of Appeal and another before the House of Lords. These cases will focus on those scenarios which do not involve spouses, merely the settlor or their children.

Example 1: *Bulmer et al v IRC*[15]

This case reached the Chancery Division of the High Court and was pursued under Income Tax Act 1952 s.404-415, an early incarnation of the present legislation. The question here was whether the relevant transactions constituted an 'arrangement'.

The appellants were a group of shareholders in a limited company ('company A'). In 1954, another unrelated (but 'friendly') limited company ('company B') established and held the shares of a subsidiary company ('company C'). The appellants sold their shares in company A to company C at a value much lower than market value, with the purchase price being held as an interest-free loan. At the same time, Company B loaned £250,000 to company C at 5% interest to buy more shares in company A to defeat a potential third-party takeover, which they did in tranches until 1961. The appellants had an option to buy back their original shares (along with those subsequently bought by company C) once that loan from company B had been paid off (which it eventually was).

The IR's initial argument was that the appellants had never relinquished the equitable interest in their company A shares to company C under s.415; as such the dividends arising from those shares should be taxable (under surtax liability) on the appellants and not company C. However, by the time the appeal reached the High Court, the IR's argument was restricted to the shares and subsequent accretions' being held on trust for Company C by the appellants due to a 'settlement' having been established by the transactions under s.411. They also argued that there was a power to revoke the settlement within s.404 such that the appellants would become beneficially entitled to the shares and could do so within six years.

The appellants argued that there was no settlement, rather it was a commercial transaction with no element of bounty; the appellants sold their shares for an agreed price and thus there was no settlement. They argued in the alternative: that if there was a settlement there was no power of revocation; that no party to the settlement had any interest in the income, or that Company B was in fact the settlor of any such settlement.

---

[15][1967] 1 Ch 145

In April 1963, the Special Commissioners concluded that there was indeed a settlement with the appellants as settlors who had provided the trust property under s.409; they had directly provided the shares and indirectly provided the accretions. As a result of this, the appellants were therefore subject to surtax liability on the shares' dividends. The appellants appealed to the High Court and the case appeared before Pennycuick J.

The judge examined the verdicts from other older settlements cases, one of which was *IRC v. Leiner*,[16] in which Plowman J had stated:

> *"it is common ground that it is implicit in the fasciculus of sections of which section 401 forms part that some element of bounty is necessary to make the sections apply and that a bona fide commercial transaction would be excluded from their operation"*

Directly adopting that approach, Pennycuick J stated:

> *"So in that case, Plowman J... proceeded on the premise that the sections before him applied only to a transaction which is not a bona fide commercial transaction. It seems to me that I ought to adopt the premise on which the two decisions which I have cited proceed and treat the section as inapplicable to a bona fide commercial transaction"*[17]

Taking this view and applying it to the present case:

> *"It seems to me abundantly clear that the transactions between the appellants and Sanderson (company B) was indeed a bona fide commercial transaction. Again, in case that imports in any respect a difference test, it is clear that there was no element of bounty between the appellants and Sanderson".*[18]

Therefore, there was no need to examine whether a 'settlement' had been created and what the terms were; the legislation only applies at all if the transaction is not on a commercial basis and where no element of bounty was involved i.e. there was no income gifting motivation. These are the overriding criteria to determine whether a settlement has been created.

Example 2: *Crossland v. Hawkins*[19]

Jack Hawkins (1910-1973) was a well-known stage and screen actor. He often portrayed military characters but was also subject to a settlements legislation dispute with IR involving his children. One arm of the settlements legislation

---

[16](1964) 41 TC 589

[17][1967] 1 Ch 145 at 164

[18]Ibid at 165-166

[19][1961] Ch 537

applies when a person's minor unmarried child can benefit from an arrangement of which they are a settlor. In his case, there was an express trust set up for the benefit of his children. Jack Hawkins' father-in-law was the legal settlor, but IR argued that Jack Hawkins was the actual settlor of a trust for his minor children thus making him taxable on their income.

A limited company was set up in 1954 through which Mr Hawkins provided his services. Of the 100 shares in the company, one went to the accountant, another to Mrs Hawkins and the remaining 98 to a trust of which Mr Hawkins's children and future issue were beneficiaries. Mr Hawkins was a director of the company but did not hold any shares. In 1955, Mr Hawkins' father-in-law settled £100 of his own money into the trust fund which bought those remaining 98 company shares. Mr Hawkins knew about this arrangement, devised by the lawyers and accountants, but was not actively involved in any of the meetings and nor was he consulted. I look at this element of knowledge below.

Jack Hawkins had signed a service agreement with the company. In the year to 30 April 1957, Mr Hawkins stared in the film *Fortune is a Woman* for which the company was paid £25,000; however, Mr Hawkins was only paid £900 by the company (a fraction of what was later called the *"enviable salary"*[20] which an actor would ordinarily earn). The remainder of the funds was declared as a dividend and the trustees subsequently distributed those monies to the beneficiaries. When income tax repayment claims were made on behalf of the children, IR denied those claims.

IR contended that: the formation of a limited company, the subsequent service agreement, the settlement of the trust and the trustees' acquisition of the shares, all constituted a single 'arrangement' under the Income Tax Act 1952. As Mr Hawkins had indirectly contributed to the settlement by the fruits of his labours materialising as dividends paid from artificially bloated company reserves (due to his low salary), he was the settlor of a trust from which his children had benefitted. Under s.397 of the 1952 Act, as settlor, he was therefore taxable upon his children's income. At the time of earning the money, Mr Hawkins knew that his fees would ultimately make their way to the trust and his children – he was a director of the company and knew about the overall objective of the arrangement.

Mr Hawkins contended that the use of a limited company was common for high earners and that the intention was to spread the burden of surtax rather than settle assets upon his children (the attitude towards tax avoidance was

---

[20] By Donovan LJ

clearly more liberal in the late 50s than it is today). Another argument was that, for an arrangement to have been in place, there must have been contemplation of the whole arrangement from the outset.

IR suffered an early blow as the General Commissioners unanimously held there was no arrangement and that Jack Hawkins was not settlor of the trust. The Chancery Division of High Court also held in favour of Mr Hawkins. Danckwerts J held that he was not settlor of the trust as a matter of fact and law, that he had contributed nothing to the trust and that the limited company and service agreement were formed before the trust, so could not form part of any unitary arrangement. IR appealed and the matter went before the Court of Appeal.

Donovan LJ pointed out that:

> "*Hawkins was not going to make a present of his services, less £50 a week, to two clerks in his solicitor's office, who on the face of things were at the beginning the only shareholders in the company. At some time he would want to have the money which had escaped surtax for himself, for example, in a liquidation of the company, or to bestow it on others whom he wished to benefit, for example, his family. Otherwise, the whole operation was pointless.*
>
> *I will accept for the moment the proposition that the family settlement which followed was not decided upon at the outset; but what is important, I think, is that the eventual enjoyment by some individual or individuals of the money which had escaped surtax must have been in contemplation at the outset. Otherwise, as I say, the scheme had no rational purpose".[21]*

Donovan LJ went on the find that there was an arrangement from the outset and that Income Tax Act 1952 s.397 does not require the whole eventual outcome to have been contemplated. Whilst conceding that the family settlement itself was not contemplated from the outset, there was clearly an overall plan from the outset to see that the children would benefit from Mr Hawkins's earnings:

> "*I think there is sufficient unity about the whole matter to justify it being called an arrangement for this purpose, because, as I have said, the ultimate object is to secure for somebody money free from what would otherwise be the burden or the full burden of surtax. Merely because the final step to secure this objective is left unresolved at the outset, and decided on later, does not seem to me to rob the scheme of the necessary unity to justify it being called an "arrangement." Particularly is this so in a case such as the present, when*

---

[21][1961] Ch 537 at 547

IMPLIED TRUSTS

one recalls certain other features of it. Thus, Hawkins, though not on the register of members, was a director of the company. He entered into this contract for services for a consideration which is a fraction in value of what he gives to the company in return. He, as a director, has to agree to the issue of the 98 shares to the trustees: he as a director has to agree to the interim dividend of £500, free of tax, being paid on this £100 of capital".[22]

The fact that Mr Hawkins was a director of the company clearly played a big part in this as far as the Court of Appeal is concerned. If he was not party to the formation of the company and trust, he was consulted and as director he would have authorised the issue of the 98 shares to the trust knowing full well that his children would benefit. Clearly too, Mr Hawkins contributed indirectly to the settlement; he hadn't put in the initial £100 settlement, but the dividends from the company came from payment for his work as an actor, which in turn made their way to his children via the trust.

Holroyd-Pearce LJ concurred. He also addressed the issue of Mr Hawkins' lack of active involvement in the company and trust:

"The mere fact that he did not concern himself with some of the "steps" in the legal machinery involved does not make it any the less his arrangement within the section. A man does not avoid the incidence of section by merely being absent from and leaving to his solicitors and accountants certain parts of the legal machinery if he is aware of the proposals for an " arrangement " or a settlement and actively forwards them by personally carrying out and assisting in the vital parts in which his performance and co-operation are necessary. Nor can he avoid liability by merely giving his solicitors carte blanche to affect some scheme for the benefit of his family and refusing to concern himself with its precise form".[23]

The Court of Appeal therefore allowed IR's appeal.

Example 3: *IRC v. Mills*[24]

Another well-known actor who fell foul of the settlements legislation (again within the Income Tax Act 1952) was the child star Hayley Mills (b.1946). The overall scenario i.e. a trust holding limited company shares, was much the same as that for Jack Hawkins. There was also a discussion about knowledge and capacity because at the time of the 'arrangement', unlike Jack Hawkins, Hayley Mills was still a minor.

---

[22]Ibid at 550

[23]Ibid at 553

[24][1975] AC 38 (HL)

In 1960, Miss Mills signed a service contract with a limited company and the following year that company signed a contract with Walt Disney Productions to provide personal services directly to the latter for five years for an annual salary of £400. The limited company was founded by Miss Mills' father (Sir John) who was anxious to shield his daughter from the pressures of a film career. He transferred the shares into a trust, which he had settled in the same year, with Miss Mills as the sole beneficiary to receive the funds absolutely at age 25. The funds (£30,000 per year initially) which flowed from Walt Disney into the trust via the limited company was assessed upon Miss Mills for years 1962-65 inclusive due to her being the effective settlor of the trust under Income Tax Act 1952 s.411 as the income had originated from her. The fact that the funds were undistributed from the trust was irrelevant. The Special Commissioners upheld the assessments as did the High Court.

However, in 1972, the Court of Appeal allowed Miss Mills' appeal. It was not a unanimous judgment though, Orr LJ held that she was a settlor. His view was that there was sufficient evidence to show that Miss Mills had 'provided' funds with intention to do so for the 'purposes of the settlement'. However, Lord Denning MR made his judgment based upon Miss Mills' age (14 at the time) and thus her inability to show sufficient understanding behind the 'purpose' or even the documents she signed, so the doctrine of 'non est factum'[25] applied. Buckley LJ too stated that there must be a motivating intention to benefit those interested under the trust. The IR took the matter to the House of Lords.

The three questions before them were: 1. did Miss Mills provide funds directly or indirectly? If so, 2. did she do so for the purposes of the settlement? And if so, 3. did the income arising in the settlement originate from her?

As to the first question: in the Court of Appeal, Lord Denning MR had held that the funds had come from the limited company; but the House of Lords disagreed. Citing Jack Hawkins' case, Viscount Dilhorne pointed out that this was taking too narrow a view of an arrangement:

---

[25]'It is not my deed', a common-law defence claiming that what was signed was fundamentally different from what was understood and therefore a mistake had been made due to ignorance. This makes the contract void ab initio.

IMPLIED TRUSTS

"To do so means shutting one's eyes to the fact that the source of the dividends was money paid for by Miss Mills' work and money which but for the arrangement would have been received by her"[26]

As for the second question, purposes of the settlement (along with the motives and intentions), we look at in the next section. However, as for the third question, the House of Lords held that:

"As Miss Hayley Mills indirectly provided income for the settlement, that income has to be treated as income originating from her and so as income arising under the settlement in which Miss Mills has an interest"[27]

The House of Lords thus found in favour of IR.

In this respect, it was the same as that for Jack Hawkins i.e. both their earning powers were being channelled through a limited company, whose profits were artificially inflated by the actors' taking a far lower salary than they would otherwise receive. From the company, the dividends went into an express trust from which the actors themselves or their children could benefit. Those express trusts each had a legal settlor, but the courts imposed another trust in place of that express trust; these implied trusts each had a new settlor designated by the court. Whilst the authorisation behind this implied trust is the settlements legislation (which has changed little in nearly 100 years), that legislation itself stems from equitable principles of beneficial ownership of the income.

6.2.5 Ingredients of the settlement legislation – is an implied trust being imposed?

The settlements legislation is one of the oldest examples of the courts' imposing an implied trust in line with equitable principles of overriding common law and recognising beneficial owners of income. However, we should tie this statement back to the analysis of implied trusts earlier in this book. Is it right to say that the settlements legislation applies an implied trust? If so, what sort?

As the trust is being imposed by a piece of anti-avoidance legislation, like that for TOAA, it is tempting to call this implied settlor-interest trust a type of constructive trust. It is created by operation of law to right a perceived wrong, the artificial transfer of the income to a person other than the beneficial owner. An implied trust is put in place as before: the beneficial

---

[26][1975] AC 38, at page 52

[27]Ibid at page 54

owner of the income is taxed upon it, the legal owner of the income is still the express trust beneficiary (as in Jack Hawkins and Hayley Mills' cases). The additional feature of this implied trust is that the settlor - as creator of that income - is also the beneficiary (or spouse or children), hence a settlor-interested trust.

However, a central ingredient of a constructive trust is the knowledge of the parties involved. The law imposes a constructive trust because it would be unconscionable to allow whatever has happened to continue; good conscience forbids it. However, if a party is involved in the arrangement in good faith then they will not have the burden of trusteeship imposed upon them. As far as the settlements legislation is concerned, as stated above, it is the position of the settlor which is significant, more so than that of the implied trustee. Should an individual be imposed with settlor status if he also enters into an arrangement in good faith and with a clear conscience? According to equitable principles, the answer would be no. In the cases of Jack Hawkins, Hayley Mills and *Donovan & McLaren*[28] the courts examined the question of the (supposed) settlor's knowledge.

In *Donovan*, the motivation behind the repeated dividend waivers was examined to ascertain whether there was a commercial basis to it all. Guidance was taken from the *Arctic Systems* case and concluded that a specific intention to avoid tax is largely irrelevant but is material in considering whether the 'arrangement' falls within the statutory definition as a planned and deliberate action or series of actions (or has sufficient 'unity' as it was called in *Crossland v. Hawkins*):[29]

> *"An intention to avoid tax is not, I think, absolutely essential. It is possible to imagine that an arrangement planned for some other purpose (such as pre-empting the consequences of insolvency or divorce) could unexpectedly prove efficacious for tax avoidance and amount to an arrangement (and so to a settlement). But usually an intention to avoid or minimise tax can readily be inferred (in this case it was candidly admitted) and that intention is part of the factual material that has to be looked at in the round"*[30]

The element of intention, according to the FTT in *Donovan* and the House of Lords in *Jones v. Garnett*, is not a vital ingredient with the settlements legislation. Indeed, the legislation makes no allowance for a subjective

---

[28][2014] UKFTT 048 (TC)

[29]Per Donavon LJ at page 549

[30][2007] 1 WLR 2030 at page 2042 per Lord Walker

IMPLIED TRUSTS

element of intent or recklessness; there is no express 'motive' defence as there is in the TOAA legislation[31]. However, intention is clearly relevant when deciding whether the scenario in front of the court meets the definition of a 'settlement' under the legislation.

In Jack Hawkins' case, the Lord Justices focused upon his personal involvement in establishing the trust and company. Whilst he was a director of the limited company, he had no shareholding and was not involved in any of the decision-making behind setting up the structure. Although he was not consulted, he knew what was going on, so there is no question of his pleading ignorance; indeed, the court held that he must have been aware of the overall aim behind the service agreement which gave the settlement the 'unity' referred to by Donavon LJ with Holroyd-Pearce LJ's statement above.

Hayley Mills' case had an interesting twist to it as she was only 14 years old at the time the trust and company were established so there was a question about whether, as a minor, she was legally capable of understanding what was going on (thus rendering the service contract she signed voidable). Indeed, in the Court of Appeal Lord Denning MR's verdict to reverse the High Court's decision was based on non est factum in that Ms Mills had no understanding of what she was signing. Her lack of any intention, let alone any malevolence, was clearly a major factor. On that point the case was distinguished with Jack Hawkins' case insofar as he at least knew what was going on; Hayley Mills had no such knowledge:

> *"The knowledge and intention that were relevant in Hawkins was that when he entered into the service agreement he knew that there was going to be a settlement".*[32]

This also had an impact on Miss Mills' providing funds for the 'purpose' of the settlement; 'purpose' implies an element of intention, foresight... or at least some knowledge of what is happening with the funds.

The House of Lords had held that Hayley Mills was the effective settlor in her case. They held that she was legally capable of entering into a service contract as there was no element of prejudice to the minor. As to the matter of intention, the Court of Appeal had held that an element of intention was necessary when considering the question about settlements; but the House of Lords dismissed this view. They pointed out that motive and intention

---

[31] ITA 2007 ss 737-742A

[32] [1973] Ch 225 (CA); per Buckley LJ at page 233

were entirely irrelevant; but in saying so, Viscount Dilhorne used a particularly unusual phrase within a civil court; he stated that:

> "I do not consider it incumbent, in order to establish that a person is a settlor as having provided funds for the purpose of a settlement, to show that there was any element of _mens rea_".[33]

'Mens rea' is a criminal law concept, meaning 'guilty mind', usually required alongside a guilty act ('actus reus') for a successful conviction. It is interesting that these words were used; it cannot be said of any Law Lord, let alone a former Lord Chancellor (which Viscount Dilhorne was between 1962-64), that they would confuse basic and fundamental criminal and civil law concepts. The 'motive' and 'intention' referred to in the Mills case is that of avoiding paying surtax through an arrangement. That is tax avoidance, to artificially transfer the income to someone paying tax at a lower rate; but it is not a crime, like tax evasion. Whilst the term used by Viscount Dilhorne was not strictly the correct one to use in a civil court, the meaning behind his sentiment was entirely understood in that the intention concerned an undesirable act and one which the legislation had been introduced to combat and therefore the deemed settlor had a guilty mind in that respect – just not in a criminal way.

It seems, therefore, that whilst explicit intention to avoid tax may not be necessary to implement the legislation, there must be some element of knowledge, awareness, or understanding as to the circumstances which prevents the individual concerned from acting in good faith or claiming they had no notice of what was happening. Having this knowledge, awareness or understanding would therefore be inherent in an 'agreement' or 'arrangement' per the legislation. The essential criterion of a clear conscience within equity is therefore still intact.

6.3 Issues with a spouse

A common scenario is one whereby a husband (and traditionally it has been a husband) diverts income to his wife as a co-shareholder/partner in a business. The cases above concerned an express trust whereby the beneficiary was either the deemed settlor herself (in Hayley Mills' case, as she was the source of the income), or his minor children (Jack Hawkins' case). However, the same piece of legislation applies if the settlor's spouse (the modern definition of which includes civil partners) is a beneficiary.

---

[33] Page 52

IMPLIED TRUSTS

6.3.1 Statutory spousal exemption

There is (and has been for some time) a specific 'get out' clause when the income is being 'gifted' to the spouse, in which case the legislation will not apply. In the modern legislation it lies in ITTOIA 2005 s.626:

> "(1) The rule in section 624(1) does not apply in respect of an outright gift —
>
> > (a) of property from which income arises,
> >
> > (b) made by one spouse to the other, and
> >
> > (c) meeting conditions A and B.
>
> (2) Condition A is that the gift carries a right to the whole of the income.
>
> (3) Condition B is that the property is not wholly or substantially a right to income".

The legislation will still apply, therefore, if <u>pure income</u> is being diverted to a spouse; however, it allows for income <u>derived from an underlying asset also gifted</u> to be taxed upon the recipient spouse. This latter scenario is the one sought after by conditions A and B above. The gift of any underlying asset itself between spouses is usually outside the scope of tax generally; for CGT purposes the gain is treated as NIL for spouses living together as such and both inter vivos and death transfers to spouses are exempt from IHT.

Prior to ITTOIA 2005, this same spousal exemption was contained within ICTA 1988 s.660A(6).

6.3.2 What is the significance of the spousal exemption to the settlements legislation?

An interesting quote about the logic behind the spousal exemption can be found within the *Patmore* case where Judge Mosedale said:[34]

> "It may at first glance seem illogical that statute allows an exemption for giving away capital from which income is derived (such as a gift of shares) but not the lesser gift of just the income. Although not necessary for my decision, I assume that this is because Parliament wished to allow a person to entirely divest themselves of property in favour of their spouse so that for all purposes separate taxation would then apply. What Parliament did not want is for a spouse to decide year on year that his or her income could be given to the spouse in order to get a lower rate of tax."

Of particular interest is the point about separate taxation i.e. the notion that each individual is taxed upon their own income/capital gains rather than as one marital unit – the latter concept is known as 'aggregation'. The USA,

---

[34][2010] TC 00619, at paragraph 75, see more below

Republic of Ireland, France, Israel, Luxembourg, Norway and Switzerland are amongst the major nations whose married couples can file jointly and thus be treated as one family unit (in France, income from children is also brought into the aggregated assessment). But in the UK and most other OECD countries, every individual is only taxed separately, regardless of their marital status.

The settlements legislation, as far as spousal scenarios are concerned, effectively flies in the face of the principle of separation by taxing one spouse's income together with that of the other spouse. HMRC will believe that the income going to the other spouse belongs to the other, and so separation is undone in the name of tackling tax-avoidance. The settlements legislation effectively encapsulates the principle of aggregation, which was at the centre of the UK tax system from the beginning. The spousal clause is the exception to that and was brought in by Finance Act 1989 s.108 following the abolition of aggregation in the Finance Act1988. The settlements legislation is a throwback to aggregation – the spousal exemption clause is the only way out. It only applies to spouses and civil partners and not to other family members (this is a wider question, and other issues exposed by the spousal exemption will be discussed below). It is drafted to ensure that generosity of gifts between spouses in maintained, but at the same time ensuring that the income splitting, the fear of which was a justification for aggregation, is discouraged.

In the *Arctic Systems* case, whilst before the Court of Appeal, Carnwath LJ pointed out the anachronism of the settlements legislation in relation to the principle of separate taxation:

> "Like Park J and Sir Andrew Morritt C, I find it odd that in this context spouses are still treated by s.660A(2) as sharing the same interest, notwithstanding their separate treatment for other income tax purposes"[35]

Sir Andrew Morritt C had said:[36]

> "Before the de-aggregation for tax purposes of the income of a married woman from that of her husband effected in 1990, this case could not have arisen because the income of Mrs Jones would have been aggregated with that of Mr Jones whether or not there would have been a settlement.... the provision of s.660A(2) may appear anachronistic, but they were not amended in 1989"

---

[35][2006] 1 WLR 1123 at 1151

[36]*ibid* at 1144

The spousal exemption is therefore a modern invention of necessity, to help mitigate the tax avoidance dangers (i.e. income splitting) now present between spouses with separate taxation, but which were not an issue in the days of aggregation.

6.3.3   History of aggregation in the UK

Aside from the settlements legislation, aggregation used to be the default method of income tax assessment by the IR for married couples. The husband was taxed upon the combined amount earned by him and his wife as per ICTA 1988 s.279. This concept began when income tax began and only ended in the UK in 1990 (per Finance Act 1988 s.32); it began coming to an end in Jersey in January 2022, having been in place since 1928.

Under the Income Tax Act 1799, a husband was assessed and taxed as if the collective incomes of himself and his wife were his alone. The Property & Income Tax Act 1806 extended the same to business and rental profits. Gradual changes were made over the years to separate the wife's income from that of her husband. In the Income Tax Act 1842, married women came under the definition of non-taxable or 'incapacitated' persons, along with infants and the insane.[37] In 1914 a wife's income could be subject to a separate assessment, though the incomes would still be taxed together. The Finance Act 1971 allowed for a wife's earned income to be assessed separately but this would have forfeited the married man's allowance (this allowance was some measure of relief from the effects of tax on two incomes). IR would only correspond with the husband about his wife's affairs, even if the wife had initially contacted them; this practice came to an end in 1978.

In those nations where joint filing is the default, aggregation usually results in a lower overall tax liability by utilising greater allowances. In 1920, aggregation had been defended by these words by the Royal Commission[38]:

"The aggregation for Income Tax purposes of the income of husband and wife is not dependent upon any medieval conception of the subordination of women; nor is it a question of sex disability, since either partner can claim separate assessment and separate collection. The incomes are aggregated because the law of taxable capacity is the supreme law in matters of taxation, and taxable capacity is, in fact, found to depend on the amount of income that accrues to the married pair, and not upon the way in which that income

---

[37]Income Tax Act 1842 sections 41, 53 (5&6 Vict.C.35)

[38]Royal Commission on The Income Tax 1919-1920, pages 58-59

happens fortuitously to be owned by the members of the union. It is beyond question that in the immense majority of cases where the wife has separate means she contributes to the common purse either by actual merger of her income with her husband's, or by bearing expenses which in less fortunate households fall upon the husband ... We therefore recommend that the aggregation of the incomes of wife and husband should continue to be the rule."

A further commission (the Radcliffe Commission) in 1955[39] defended the policy and continued encouragement was largely based upon support for the institution of marriage and accepted that tax policy should recognise married couples as one unit accordingly. The Canadian Royal Commission in 1966 outlined the thinking behind this when it said:[40]

"Although few marriages are entered into for purely financial reasons, as soon as a marriage is contracted it is the continued income and financial position of the family which is ordinarily of primary concern, not the income and financial position of the individual members....it is probably even truer that the newly-formed family acts as a financial unit in making its expenditures. Family income is normally budgeted between current and capital outlays, and major decisions involving the latter are usually made jointly by the spouses"

Indeed, some arguments in favour of aggregation point out that doing so dissuades the individuals from using income-splitting arrangements to avoid income tax[41] i.e. it takes over the role of the settlements legislation. However, the traditional argument was simply that it makes sense to tax one family unit, where incomes are combined, as one person. Indeed, Stamp Duty Land Tax (SDLT) in England and Northern Ireland (and Land Transaction Tax in Wales) still treat a married couple as one unit as far as property purchases are concerned, as does the Higher Income Child Benefit Charge (HICBC – see chapter 6). Scotland's equivalent of SDLT, the Land & Buildings Transaction Tax (LBTT), treats cohabiting couples and dependent children the same way as married couples when considering whether the Additional Dwelling Supplement applies[42]. HMRC generally deem married couples to be living together; indeed, the CGT inter-spousal 'no-gain/no-

---

[39] Royal Commission para 119

[40] Canadian Royal Commission on Taxation, report volume 3, 123

[41] Oliver & Harris, *Comparative Perspectives on Revenue Law* (CUP 2008) chapter 11

[42] LBTT (Amendment)(Scotland) Act 2016 Schedule 2A

loss' rules require spouses to be living together for at least some point in the tax year.[43]

By the mid-1980s, there was more recognition for a change toward separate taxation in the name of greater rights and independence for wives. In his budget speech in 1985, Nigel Lawson said:

> "The present structure of personal income tax is far from satisfactory ... The system discriminates against the family in which the wife stays at home to look after the children. It denies to the partners in a marriage the independence and privacy in their tax affairs which they have a right to expect. There is therefore a strong case for changing to a new system of personal allowances more suited to today's economic and social needs. Under this, everyone, man or woman, married or single, would have the same standard allowance; but if either a wife or husband were unable to make full use of their allowance, the unused portion could be transferred, if they so wished, to their partner."

30 years later, his desire to see an element of transferable personal allowance between couples came to fruition.

Questions surrounding the family were coming to the fore; as the number of married couples fell and cohabiting couples became more common, the justification for aggregation on the grounds of marriage being the cornerstone of life gradually declined.

Finally, in 1990, nearly 200 years of aggregation ended and separate taxation between married couples became the basis of the UK direct tax system. A married person's allowance was introduced to help cushion the blow of moving to separate taxation, but that allowance only lasted a further 10 years. The move was seen largely as a movement toward greater autonomy for wives in particular; it also provided greater privacy, as previously the wife would need to disclose all her financial affairs to her husband for joint reporting. Tax planning surrounding income splitting was now possible. The settlements legislation was the only piece of legislation designed to reverse this position in the name of anti-avoidance. The government wanted a spouse to gift assets (ideally the husband gifting assets to the wife to balance ownership), but not just to artificially split income at the same time by making gifts purely of income.

---

[43]TCGA 1992 s.58

6.3.4   Cases concerning spousal exemption

Before discussing the main case, two FTT cases which involve and illustrate the spousal exemption should be highlighted. These cases actually involved dividend waivers, so would sit nicely within the section above. However, they were unable to make use of the spousal exemption clause:

Example 1: *Donovan & McLaren v. HMRC*[44]

Messrs Donovan and McLaren had been directors and shareholders of a company since 1992 and, in 2001, their wives became 10% shareholders with the directors holding 40% each.

In the company's accounting period to 31 March 2010 a total of £130,000 of dividends were paid in respect of ordinary shares:

- Mr P Donovan: £33,000 (25.38%);
- Mrs R Donovan £32,000 (24.62%);
- Mr P McLaren £33,000 (25.38%); and
- Mrs A McLaren £32,000 (24.62%).

In April 2009 the company declared an interim dividend of £3,200 per share in respect of the accounting period ended 31 March 2010. On the same date the taxpayers signed deeds of dividend waiver, waiving entitlement to the interim dividend for a period of one day. Similar actions occurred in respect of an interim dividend of £825 per share. There had been similar allocation of dividends back to the year ended 31 March 2001.

HMRC argued that the effect of the dividend waivers, and the intention of them, was to allow higher dividends to be paid to the directors' wives and that the settlements legislation applied. The directors had waived entitlement to dividends as part of a plan which constituted an arrangement with an intention to avoid tax, seeking equalisation of their dividend income.

In response to the directors' argument that the reason for the dividend waiver was to maintain reserves and cash balances to fund the purchase of the company's own freehold property, HMRC argued that if this were true, the aim could have been achieved by voting a lower dividend per share. This was not an arrangement which would have been entered into with someone at arm's length and therefore contained an element of bounty. There was no commercial purpose to the dividend waivers executed over a number of years.

---

[44] [2014] UKFTT 048 (TC)

The exemption for inter-spouse gifts did not apply as there was no outright gift but rather a dividend waiver that was declared in respect of shares.

The directors argued that that the company did have sufficient distributable reserves and so HMRC had not established that the necessary element of bounty was present. The directors had paid £1 for the shares - no actual monies were exchanged but the accounts were altered to reflect the position and, accordingly, the shares constituted a gift and fell within the inter-spouse exemption. The Tribunal stated:

"We found the irresistible inference from the facts of these appeals to be that the Appellants waived their entitlement to dividends as part of a plan to ensure that the dividend income became payable to their wives.

We were satisfied on the balance of probabilities that the intention behind the plan was tax geared to bring about a near equalisation of the Appellants' and their wives' dividend income thereby reducing their aggregate liability to Income Tax.

In reaching this decision we considered the Appellant's assertion (unsupported by evidence but set out in correspondence contained within the bundle provided to us) that the reason for executing the dividend waiver was to maintain reserves and cash balances in order to accumulate sufficient of each to fund the purchase of the company's own freehold property. On the balance of probabilities we preferred the submissions of HMRC and accepted, not least from the repeated dividend waivers over a significant number of years, that had this been the case the aim could have been achieved by other means such as voting a lower dividend per share.

We found as a fact that there was no commercial purpose for the waivers and that they would not have taken place at arm's length.

We did not find that the issue of distributable reserves was the conclusive factor on the issue of bounty and we noted that in Buck Sir Stephen Oliver QC considered the point after making a determination on the issue of bounty which corroborated our view that it was not, in isolation, conclusive. However, to the extent that it is relevant we preferred the evidence of HMRC on the matter. We noted that the figures exhibited within the bundle provided to us which demonstrated that the company only held sufficient reserves if the earlier years' waivers were taken into account, were taken from the company accounts and we accepted that they reflected the picture accurately. We took the view that to view the figures by ignoring previous waivers was artificial and that the cumulative effect of the arrangements should not be ignored. In those circumstances we found that there was a lack of sufficient distributable reserves within the company were it not for the Appellants waiving the dividends.

...even if we were to accept that there had been a gift of the shares, we were satisfied that the instant appeals still do not fall within the exception."

Their appeals were dismissed.

Example 2: *Buck v. HMRC*[45]

As well as being director, Mr Buck owned 9,999 shares in a company with 10,000 issued shares. Mrs Buck owned the remaining single share. Profits for the year ended 31 March 1999 were £35,707 and a dividend of £35,000 for Mr Buck was waived. As a result of these waivers by Mr Buck, Mrs Buck received gross dividends on her single share of £39,371 and £27,774 for years ending 1999 and 2000 respectively. Had that same level of dividends been paid on all shares, the company's distributable reserves would need to have been in the region of £300million.

HMRC's argument was therefore self-explanatory. Clearly there had been a settlement on uncommercial terms and as (like with Donovan above) Mrs Buck had received only a gift of income, the spousal exemption was not valid. Perhaps to make matters worse, Mr Buck did not attend the appeal when it came before the Special Commissioners. When asking themselves whether the same arrangement would have taken place on an arm's length basis, the Commissioners held that the state of the company's distributable reserves meant that such an arrangement could never have taken place on a commercial basis – indeed would have been impossible. The gift was clearly purely income as she received no shares as part of the gift.

Dividend waivers are rarely going to succeed in coming under the spousal exemption because they are, almost by definition, gifts of pure income. One person's waiving a dividend means someone else is ultimately, eventually able to receive it instead; this extra dividend has no extra shareholding to underlie it, so it is pure extra income. Aside from any question from spousal exemption, repeated and/or large waiver use is going to attract the attention of HMRC. There is little commercial justification in giving a dividend to someone else; it is gift of income, a benevolent act as it is a means of diverting income from one person to another – precisely the thing that the legislation was designed to prevent, even between spouses.

Turning to the most significant settlements case of recent years...

---

[45][2009] STC (SCD) 6

IMPLIED TRUSTS

Jones v. Garnett[46] ('Arctic Systems') concerned a husband and wife who were both receiving dividends as 50:50 shareholders in their company. The issue for IR/HMRC, was the fact that the husband only took a salary of £6,520 in the relevant year (1999/2000), way below a commercial salary for an IT consultant like him. As a result of this, the distributable reserves within the company were artificially inflated with half subsequently being distributed to his wife (£25,767 each).

By forming the company, transferring a share to his wife, taking the lower salary and distributing dividends to his wife, IR said Mr Jones had created a settlement and so his wife's income was taxable on him. Even if that were not the case, IR said that the gift to his wife was wholly or substantially a right to income and therefore outside the reach of the spousal exemption.

Mr Jones argued his wife had acquired her share for value and made a contribution to the business. He also said that there was no arrangement insofar as her receiving dividends was concerned as that was entirely dependent on future performance of the business, so there was no element of bounty which is a key criterion. In any event, the spousal exemption applied because the gift to his wife was a share which not only conferred dividends, but also provided a right to vote, to block resolutions or to receive assets upon winding up etc. The income she received was derived from an underlying capital asset.

The case made its way to the House of Lords, the High Court having accepting IR's argument, but the Court of Appeal overturned that judgement. The House of Lords agreed that there was indeed a settlement as summed up by Lord Hoffman:

> "I cannot agree that this was a 'normal commercial transaction between two adults'. It made sense only on the basis that the two adults were married to each other. If Mrs Jones had been a stranger offering her services as a bookkeeper, it would have been a most abnormal transaction. It would not have been an arrangement into which Mr Jones would ever have entered with someone with whom he was dealing at arms' length. It was only 'natural love and affection' which provided the consideration for the benefit he intended to confer upon his wife. That is sufficient to provide the necessary 'element of bounty'."

---

[46][2007] 1 WLR 2030

So, whilst IR won that round, it lost overall because the Lords agreed with Mr Jones that he had successfully deployed the spousal exemption clause within (at the time) ICTA 1988 s.660(6).

This case is often cited as one of the pivotal settlements cases, but in many respects it isn't really – the Joneses fell foul of the legislation in the same way as Jack Hawkins did (whose case was frequently cited by IR). What is interesting about this case is that it was the spousal exemption that saved them (coupled to the fact it was the House of Lords who did so). Mrs Jones had not received a gift of pure income like Mrs McLaren and Mrs Buck did; the underlying shares essentially saved Mrs Jones' position. The 1990 change followed the policy of the wider UK tax system which encouraged the gift of income-producing capital assets from husband to wife – the IHT and CGT provisions echo this – but it is the splitting and gifting of pure income which Parliament clearly disapproves of, and they have used implied trusts to impose a pre-1990 position for spouses.

Following the House of Lords' decision in *Arctic Systems*, the government launched a consultation in December 2007 on changing the law to effectively overrule that decision.[47] Draft legislation was drawn up accordingly, but it was subsequently withdrawn. No further legislative action has been taken since.

6.3.5 What other issues does the spousal exemption expose besides that of implied trusts?

One question is: why does the exemption only apply to spouses? More and more couples are choosing to cohabit rather than marry, yet they would not benefit from the current exemption. Tiley[48] cites that whilst fewer than one in 100 adults under 50 were cohabiting in the early 1960s, by 2007 it was one in six. In tax generally there are no provisions for cohabitating couples; the IHT and CGT exemption provisions only extend to married couples and civil partners living together as such. The spousal exemption question therefore comes under a much wider question about society and cohabitees' rights.

The other question, which addresses aggregation more than the spousal exemption specifically is: how does this impact on tax benefits, such as tax credits and child benefit? Commentators[49] have taken the issue of tax credits and applied it to the principle of aggregation; and child benefit is now

---

[47]"Income Shifting: a consultation on draft legislation"

[48]*Tiley's Revenue Law*, 9th Ed, Hart 2019

[49]E.g. David Salter

assessed on a household level to ascertain whether the HICBC should apply. Along with the settlements legislation itself, these things contradict the principle of separate taxation. Tiley argues[50] that the tax system actually works as a disincentive to marriage: as well as the child benefit issue (see below), only one property is available for CGT Principal Private Residence relief (PPR) for a married couple, whereas cohabiting couples could have one property each gaining the benefit of PPR.

The Tax Credit system (introduced in 2003) is based upon couples' "*living together as husband and wife or as civil partners*",[51] which can include unmarried couples (sometimes known, incorrectly, as 'common law spouses'); so HMRC need to ask themselves whether an unmarried couple are indeed living together as husband and wife. Why, Tiley asks,[52] could the same definition not apply to the wider tax system? To the IHT exemption? To the spousal exemption within the settlements legislation?

The child benefit system underwent significant change in January 2013 when the HICBC came into being. Anyone whose adjusted net income exceeded £50,000 would have their child benefit clawed back through the self-assessment system, until it disappeared completely once earnings reached £60,000. Aside from the issue of introducing self-assessment tax returns to a completely tax-unrelated matter, the basis of assessment being influenced by combined household income goes against the principle of separate taxation. The HICBC is brought into effect for the person claiming the benefit (usually the mother) but it is affected by anyone in the household earning more than £50,000. So, we have the totally unsatisfactory situation where, on one extreme, we could have one person in the house earning nothing and another earning £60,000 resulting in 100% of the child benefit being clawed back; conversely if both parties earned £49,999 each (and thus a larger total household income) there would be no clawback. A system which respects the principle of separate taxation would assess the recipient of the payment exclusively; however, the HICBC assumes that a couple will pool their income, which was the main argument in favour of aggregation in the first place.

Clearly, therefore, the concept of separation of couples for other non-tax purposes is far from absolute; as far as social security is concerned, both the

---

[50]In his article: "Tax, Marriage and the Family" CJL 2006 65(2)

[51]Tax Credit Act 2002 s3(5A)

[52]In *Tiley's Revenue Law*, 9th Ed, Hart 2019, page 179; also in his article "Tax, Marriage and the Family" CJL 2006 65(2)

tax credit system and (to some extent) the HICBC revert back to the principle of aggregation in assessing a couple within a household.

A wider question though remains about the recognition by the tax system of families and couples. That is a topic for discussion in its own right, and I will not go into it in any detail here. However, it is worth a brief examination in respect of the spousal position within the tax system. For example, consider siblings and IHT.

Currently only spouses and civil partners can benefit from the IHT spousal transfer exemption.[53] In 2008, two sisters, Joyce and Sybil Burden, took the government to the European Court of Human Rights to argue that the law was discriminatory. They had been left land by their father and, as they were both unmarried, wished to leave their share of the land to each other upon first death; however, their being siblings mean such a bequest would not qualify as an exempt transfer. Their claim was defeated by the court. On 14 January 2020, the first reading took place in the House of Lords of a Private Members' Bill,[54] tabled by Conservative peer Lord Lexden, which seeks to amend the current IHT spousal exemption to include siblings who have lived together for at least seven years and provided the surviving sibling is over 30 years old. This Bill follows a similar case to the Burdens', namely that of sisters Catherine and Virginia Utley who wanted to enter into a civil partnership so they could take advantage of the IHT spousal exemption upon first death so that IHT would not be chargeable upon the south London home they owned together. Siblings of half-blood would also qualify under the proposed amendment.

More generally, the Lower Income Tax Reform Group within the Chartered Institute of Taxation published a report in 2015[55] looking at the definition of couples on issues such as universal credit, bereavement payments, child benefit and married couple's allowance. The report points out that:

"There are a number of potential relationships that could warrant the label of a 'couple'. The easiest to identify and agree in terms of definition are married couples and civil partners, and those physically and emotionally living together as if they were a married couple or civil partners. But increasingly,

---

[53]IHTA 1984 s.18. Unlike with the CGT no-gain/no-loss rule which merely neutralises the tax, the IHT equivalent is a blanket exemption; it also does not require spouses to be living together as such.

[54]Inheritance Tax Act 1984 (Amendment) (Siblings) Bill [HL] 2019-21

[55]"Couples in the tax and related welfare systems – a call for greater clarity" May 2015 at page 7

people are living in other ways including 'living apart together' (that is, a couple who are emotionally committed but physically live separately either some or all of the time). There are also those who used to be part of a couple but whose emotional relationship has ended, yet they remain living under the same roof (usually enforced for practical reasons such as sharing childcare, or financial constraints). These additional categories make defining who is and is not part of a couple more complicated.

While it is possible to define various potential categories of couple, within each category of couple there are nevertheless shades of grey, making it difficult to determine the boundaries of the various categories. These include the differing degrees to which people share their lives together, and a particular difficulty as to timing – when does a couple's relationship become sufficiently cemented such that they are 'living together as a married couple'; and when have a couple finally become separated at the end of their relationship? Often there is no clear start or end date".

Social models change over time; they always have done, and obviously the tax regime needs to fit into that. Until the end of aggregation, this was based on treating husband and wife as one unit; but for HICBC the basis of assessment is essentially on individuals within a household. As far as SDLT in concerned, aggregation is practically still in force, as married couples are treated as one unit; but Scotland has gone further with LBTT's (limited) treatment of cohabitees and married couples the same, despite the potential difficulties with definitions. Within the TOAA legislation, *"persons living together"* are equated to spouses/civil partner where payments are received by non-UK resident 'settlors' or their spouses.[56] Tax reliefs on transactions between two individuals are still only in place for married couple/civil partners, rather than households or non-married couples.

It would certainly seem reasonable to revisit the issue of non-married couples' reliefs and to decide whether we should have tax assessments on a purely individual basis or as family units. If couples/households are to form the basis of any area of taxation then, as the above report says, the definitions of 'couples' or 'cohabitees' should be made clear.

---

[56]ITA 2007 s.731(1B)b)

7 How did equity and beneficial ownership find their way into the courts in the first place? And how did this affect tax?

"Equity was a system of curial remedies which evolved in England in the fifteenth century in the Court of the Lord Chancellor. It was, like any other system, fundamentally a combination of the theoretical principles of justice and the practical problems of putting them into operation"[1]

This is an important question because it is the law of equity which creates a beneficial interest. The common law would only recognise legal titles so the concept that someone else could be the 'real' or beneficial owner was born out of the law of conscience and equity. The ability of the modern courts to recognise the existence of beneficial ownership through any form of trust is therefore down to equitable principles' being inherent within its jurisdiction.

The statement by W H Bryson above really sums up equity as a remedial and supervisory force to common law. It stemmed from the discretion of the courts as a means of trying to resolve problems before them in a way which would be just and equitable. Before then the King himself, or rather his own Council (the 'Curia Regis'), would receive petitions for relief from individuals who were shackled by the inflexibility of the common law. The Lord Chancellor would review these petitions as a member of the Curia Regis, head of the royal judiciary and of the office dealing with writs (Professor Tout referred to the Lord Chancellor as the *"King's natural prime minister"*).[2] The role was one of royal secretariat rather than a court due to the Chancellor's custodianship of the 'Great Seal' of the Realm which authenticated documents (any royal grants of property, writs and commissions in the King's name needed to 'pass the Seal of Chancery' which had been authenticating royal documents since the 11th century). Indeed, it was this Seal which gave the Chancellor his power. In the Statute of Westminster 1285, the Lord Chancellor was given the power to vary the form of Writs so that justice could be done, thus sowing the seeds of the modern laws and courts of equity.

By 1238 this role had already detached from the Curia Regis to form a separate court, but equity was not yet considered a separate body of law. Indeed, until the reign of Elizabeth I, the Chancery Court also had some

---

[1] W H Bryson *"The Equity Side of the Exchequer"* page 9

[2] Cited in *"A History of English Law"* at page 395

criminal jurisdiction, but this was gradually hived off to the common law courts and the Star Chamber (which was itself abolished in 1641 along with the Court of Requests). At this time the common law was still in its relative infancy, but equity grew alongside it to supplement and correct it when justice and equity so required. This is not a modern view in hindsight, Sir John Baker[3] reminds us that Aristotle had written in his *Ethica Nichomachea* about:

> *"'aequitas' as a means of correcting general laws, which in their nature could not provide for every eventuality and to him it meant interpreting written laws according to the intention rather than the letter"*

This would be known today as the 'purposive' approach to statutory interpretation.

Medieval lawyers would have been aware of this and considered it part and parcel of common law and its process; all courts had some undercurrent of equity flowing through them. W H Bryson[4](again) sums it up nicely:

> *"Thus did equity supplement and complement the common law. Equity does not compete with the common law but tunes it more finely. The common law is, in theory, a complete system; equity is not a system within itself but rather relates to the common law and aids the common law. English justice came to consist of both common law and equity and would be defective without both. This was recognised as early as the fifteenth century".*

What was new was equity's being administered in the form of justice overseen by the Lord Chancellor, as opposed to its being integral in the common law courts.[5] By the late 15th century, the High Court of Chancery (or 'Chancery Court') was freestanding with the Lord Chancellor having his own authority outside that of the Council or the common law courts. From 1851 the Lord Chancellor also sat on the bench in the 'Court of Appeal in Chancery', until the numerous appellate courts were merged in 1873. The House of Lords heard the first case from the equity side of the Exchequer Court (see below) in 1660,[6] with the right of the House of Lords to hear equity appeals being settled by 1677.

---

[3]In the *"Introduction of English Legal History"* at page 116

[4]In *"Cases Concerning Equity* Volume 1" by Seldon Society, page xli

[5]According to Glanvill as cited by Seldon Society ibid

[6]*Fanshawe v Impey (1660)*(11 December)

The 'Twelve Clerks' (later known as 'Masters') were the clerical officers and assistants to the Lord Chancellor; the head of this group was the 'Master of the Rolls' (properly known as 'Keeper of the Rolls of Chancery') who was the other chancery judge. He started cases and, more importantly, kept custody of the Great Seal. The Master of the Rolls had his own clerks known as the 'Six Clerks' (who operated firstly out of Chancery Lane and then 10 Stone Buildings in Lincoln's Inn from 1774 until their abolition in 1843). The Masters were themselves abolished in 1852, with the Master of the Rolls being reassigned to the new Court of Appeal in 1881 as head of the civil division. The office remains intact today as the second most powerful judicial office behind that of the Lord Chief Justice. At the time of writing, the current Master of the Rolls is Sir Geoffrey Vos. The 'Rolls', onto which Solicitors in England and Wales are admitted, are those of which the Master of the Rolls is Keeper.

The first Vice-Chancellor (Sir Thomas Plumer) was appointed in 1813 to assist the Lord Chancellor as well as the Master of the Rolls (the office to which Sir Thomas was subsequently appointed in 1818) with the increasing workload. The office of Vice-Chancellor was abolished when the Court of Chancery was itself dissolved in 1873; but it was revived again for a further 35 years in 1970.

The medieval Lord Chancellors were generally clergymen (archbishops) rather than lawyers – the concept of equity essentially being one of conscience rather than law. This did not change until Sir Thomas More's time after which the Lord Chancellors were chosen from the ranks of lawyers, Cardinal Wolsey being the last of the ecclesiastics. In the 1615 case of *Earl of Oxford*[7] Lord Ellesmere C gave the rationale behind equity:

> "that men's actions are so diverse and infinite that it is impossible to make a general law which may aptly meet with every particular and not fail in some circumstances. The office of Chancellor is to correct men's consciences for frauds, breaches of trust, wrongs, and oppressions of what nature 'soever they be, and to soften and mollify the extremity of the law"

In a chancery case of 1452, Fortescue CJ pointed out, in the face of a legal argument that *"we are to argue conscience here, not the law"*.[8] This statement sums up what chancery is all about.

---

[7] (1615) 21 ER 485

[8] Mich. 31 Hen VI. Cited in *"Introduction to English Legal History"* at page 118

IMPLIED TRUSTS

The Court of Chancery was essentially the Lord Chancellor's personal court, a one-man court which was largely swayed by the occupier's personality. This, combined with the flexible nature by which the Lord Chancellor would dispense relief to suit the individual injustice before him, led to one of the equitable maxims being *"equity of this Court varies with the length of the Chancellor's foot"*[9], usually attributed to John Selden:

> *"Equity is a roguish thing: for law we have a measure, know what to trust to; equity is according to the conscience of him that is Chancellor, and as that is larger or narrower, so is equity. 'Tis all one as if they should make the standard for the measure we call a foot, a Chancellor's foot; what an uncertain measure would this be? One Chancellor has a long foot, another a short foot, a third an indifferent foot: 'tis the same thing in a Chancellor's conscience"*[10]

Trusts came within the jurisdiction of the equitable courts because of the very nature of looking past the common law/legal owner and recognising the true and rightful owner. However, there was no recognition to that arrangement in common law - the legal owner was the only person capable of being the owner and so no writ existed to enforce the arrangement. Common law judges could not change the law to make it so, therefore the matter would be decided by the Lord Chancellor and enforced by injunctions from the courts of equity.

But what about tax in particular? The Court of Chancery concerned itself with administration of estates, jurisdiction over children's guardianship and lunatics as well as charities (i.e. estates held for charitable purposes and sale of charity land). Who had jurisdiction over tax?

7.1   Court of Exchequer

The High Court of Chancery was the Chancellor's court of equity with equitable jurisdiction over all people for all types of civil cases.

The Court of Exchequer (or 'Exchequer of Pleas') was the other equity court for much of its life, which was also originally part of the Curia Regis and also became a separate court by the late 12th century. This court originally had both common law and equitable jurisdiction until the foundation of the Court of Common Pleas (following the Magna Carta), after which it became an exclusively equitable court. Plunckett observed that:

---

[9] Per Lord Eldon C in *Gee v. Pritchard* (1818) 2 Swans 402 at 414

[10] John Selden's "Table Talk"

"the equity side of the Court of Exchequer is by far the most obscure of all the English jurisdictions".[11]

Following the Administration of Justices Act 1841, the Exchequer Court regained its common law jurisdiction and lost that of equity. Whilst it had been an equity court, unlike the Chancery Court which was open to all, the Exchequer Court's equitable jurisdiction was restricted to those matters and persons concerned with the revenue of the Crown, i.e. only the King could officially bring a case. Only officers of the Exchequer, royal accountants and informers for the King could sue in the Exchequer Court; also included in that privileged list were debtors to the Crown (i.e. taxpayers), meaning this was arguably the first 'tax court' as well as the senior equity court due to this royal jurisdiction. The name 'Exchequer' derives from the chequered cloth upon which Crown revenue was counted; it was derived from the Norman French word 'eschequier', meaning 'chessboard'. The 'upper' Exchequer became the court whose Barons were responsible for counting and collecting the taxes and who would meet twice a year to regulate the accounts; a 'lower' Exchequer (the forerunner of the Treasury) would ultimately receive these sums on behalf of the Crown. This tax role was enforced in 1541 when equitable defences could be employed in revenue actions. According to Bryson:[12]

> *"The revenue function of the Exchequer remained its primary characteristic, and from this humble origin as a tax collector, it answered the call to administer equity. Like St Matthew the Exchequer rose and went on to bigger and better things."*

Because of this revenue function, the Lord High Treasurer was the Exchequer Court's formal Head; but the Chancellor of the Exchequer (who, like the Master of the Rolls, originated from the Lord Chancellor's clerks) was another officer of the court who was also head of the Treasury in the mid-18th century, thus establishing its modern role. However, the chief clerical officer for the equity side of the Exchequer Court was the King's Remembrancer, whose office handled all Exchequer bills in equity as well as the revenue side of the court. Despite the court's being one of equity for most of its life, its Barons were drawn exclusively from the Serjeants-at-Law. These were an elite order of common law barristers in England and Ireland whose gradual demise began with the foundation of 'Queen's Counsel

---

[11] From his *"Concise History of Common Law"* (1956). Cited by W H Bryson in *"The Equity Side of the Exchequer"*

[12] *"The Equity Side of the Exchequer"* page 33

IMPLIED TRUSTS

Extraordinary' or QCs, by Elizabeth I in 1596. The Barons were on an equal footing with their common law counterparts in the Courts of Common Pleas and King's Bench.

7.2 Modern High Court

By the Victorian era, the Court of Chancery (the only court of equity from 1841) was coming under a great deal of criticism, in particular because of the costs involved, the backlogs and amount of time it took cases to make their way through. Probably the most famous contemporary example of this criticism can be found within Charles Dickens' *Bleak House* (1852-3). The novel revolves around the case of *Jarndyce v Jarndyce*, whereby a disputed inheritance is, ironically, dissipated by the legal fees of a seemingly never-ending suit in the Chancery Court. In the first chapter, it reads:

> *"Jarndyce and Jarndyce drones on. This scarecrow of a suit has, over the course of time, become so complicated, that no man alive knows what it means. The parties to it understand it least; but it has been observed that no two Chancery lawyers can talk about it for five minutes without coming to a total disagreement as to all the premises…. The little plaintiff or defendant who was promised a new rocking-horse when Jarndyce and Jarndyce should be settled has grown up, possessed himself of a real horse, and trotted away into the other world. Fair wards of court have faded into mothers and grandmothers; a long procession of Chancellors has come in and gone out"*

It seems that Dickens took inspiration from real life Chancery cases, as cited in the novel's historical context introduction. One of those concerned the will of Charles Day which started in 1834 and was still on-going at the time of the novel's writing. Another case concerned the will of William Jennings, which started in 1798 and lasted until 1878 with costs of £250,000 (nearly £30million in today's money).

When the time came for the old individual courts to be swept away with the Judicature Act 1873, their replacement was the High Court of England and Wales which we know today; thus merging (or 'fusing') the common law and equity courts into one concurrent jurisdiction – certainly insofar as one court could now administer both bodies of law. There is some debate as to whether the fusion is only procedural or whether it is also substantive, or whether it happened at all. According to Ashburner's 1954 *"Principles of Equity"*:

> *"the two streams of jurisdiction, though they run in the same channel run side by side and do not mingle their waters"*

Against Lord Diplock's stating:

"by 1977 this metaphor of two streams running side by side has in my view become both mischievous and deceptive. The innate conservatism of English lawyers made them slow to recognise that by the Supreme Court of Judicature Acts 1873 the two systems of substantive and adjectival law formerly administered by the Courts of Law and the Courts of Chancery were fused".[13]

This alludes to the idea of equitable principles' being an inherent part of the common law courts, those principles acting as a 'correcting' influence in an otherwise mono-jurisdictional court. Lord Browne-Wilkinson[14] seemed to concur with this when he said:

"The reality of the matter is that English Law has one single law of property made up of legal and equitable interests".

Whichever the school of thought, suffice it to say that the initial intention (or an initial intention) behind the change was to merge the two courts to some degree. A section from the First Report of the Judicature commission in 1869 reads:

"No suitor should be defeated because he commenced his dispute in the wrong Court, and sending the suitor from equity to law and from law to equity, to begin his suit over again in order to obtain redress, will no longer be possible …. Each division of the Supreme Court should be enabled to grant such relief or apply such remedy or combination of remedies … as all the present Courts combined would have jurisdiction to administer."

Today's High Court of Justice and the Court of Appeal (within the Royal Courts of Justice on the Strand in London) along with the Crown Courts were collectively known as the 'Supreme Court of Judicature' and renamed the 'Supreme Court of England & Wales' in 1981. However, following the creation of the 'Supreme Court of the United Kingdom' in 2009 (which assumed the judicial role of the House of Lords as the highest court of appeal), the collective term was changed to 'Senior Courts of England & Wales' to avoid any confusion.

Below the Supreme Court of the United Kingdom, Scotland and Northern Ireland retain their own system of criminal and civil courts. However, all the courts and tribunals throughout the UK are administered and overseen by HM Courts & Tribunals Service.

---

[13]*United Scientific Holdings Ltd v. Burnley Borough Council* [1978] AC 904 at 924-925

[14]In *Tinsley v. Milligan* [1994] 1 AC 340

IMPLIED TRUSTS

Following the creation of the single High Court in 1873, the trusts and tax jurisdictions of the old Chancery and Exchequer Courts respectively were represented by their own 'Divisions' within the new High Court. It was not until 1880, upon the death of the last Lord Chief Baron of the Exchequer (Fitzroy Kelly), that the Exchequer Division itself was abolished with its Common law jurisdiction absorbed into the Queen's Bench Division and that of taxation transferred to the Chancery Division.

The Lord Chancellor had assumed the position as Head of the Chancery Division until the Administration of Justice Act 1970 revived the post of Vice-Chancellor as deputy to the Lord Chancellor and placed that new officer in charge of the Chancery Division. The first new incumbent was Sir John Pennycuick; the last being Sir Andrew Morritt who was in office when the post was abolished for a second time following the Constitutional Reform Act which took effect on 1 October 2005, but the office stayed substantially the same. Indeed, Sir Andrew remained in position and resumed his duties in the successor role which was renamed the 'Chancellor of the High Court'. This is a nice reminder of where the original Lord Chancellor's judicial duties began all those centuries ago. At the time of writing, the current Chancellor of the High Court is Sir Julian Flaux following Sir Geoffrey Vos's elevation to the office of Master of the Rolls.

As well as having jurisdiction over land, trusts, insolvency, tax and probate law, the Chancery Division also concerns itself with business law and accommodates the specialist Companies Court, Patents Court and Intellectual Property Enterprise Court. The Chancery Division sits in the Rolls Building, off Fetter Lane in London.

For completion, the other divisions within the High Court are:

The King's Bench Division (KBD, the descendant of the common law Court of the King's Bench) is the largest of the three Divisions and was headed by the Lord Chief Justice until 2005 when the post became the 'President of the Queen's (now King's) Bench Division' and is currently held by Dame Victoria Sharp (the Lord Chief Justice took over the Lord Chancellor's role as Head of the Judiciary as part of the 2005 reforms). There are specialist sub-divisions within the KBD; besides the Commercial and Admiralty Court, there is the Technology & Construction Court (which evolved from the old Official Referees' Court) and the Administrative Court (in which judges from the other Divisions may sit to hear Judicial Reviews and criminal appeals). The KBD is based within the Royal Courts of Justice.

Along with the need for greater dispute resolution capacity, the overlap between the jurisdictions of the KBD and Chancery Divisions in certain matters of business and property led, in July 2017, to the creation of a specialist, unified court to hear such disputes. This 'Business & Property Court' allows judges from the various specialisms to be pooled and handle disputes arising from: Commercial and Admiralty Court cases, Technology and Constructive Court cases, insolvency, competitions, companies, intellectual property and financial lists. It also presides over those matters traditionally dealt with by the Chancery Division, including trusts, probate and revenue cases. Also included are those cases stemming from the Commercial Circuit (formerly known as the Mercantile) Courts which handled cases which sat between the jurisdictions of the KBD's Commercial Court and the Chancery Division. The Business & Property courts sit within the Rolls Building but also operate through civil courts in Leeds, Manchester, Birmingham, Cardiff and Bristol.

The Family Division as we know it today only came about in 1970 following the merger of the old Admiralty courts with the Divorce and Matrimonial Causes, into that of the 'Probate, Divorce and Admiralty' Division (the Court of *"Wills, Wives and Wrecks"* as the humourist and law reformer Sir Alan Herbert once referred to it). It was renamed the Family Division in 1970 when the responsibility for probate was assumed by the Chancery Division and when admiralty went to the KBD to combine and form the Commercial and Admiralty Court. The Family Division is now headed by the 'President of the Family Division' who is currently Sir Andrew McFarlane. Like the KBD, the Family Division is based within the Royal Courts of Justice, though the District Judges sit at First Avenue House in Holborn.

8 How are equity and beneficial ownership represented in today's laws?

"The Chancellor of the Exchequer is a man whose duties make him more or less of a taxing machine. He is intrusted with a certain amount of misery which is his duty to distribute as fairly as he can"[1]

As well as creating the Supreme Court of Judicature and unifying the two jurisdictions, one of the other things which the Judicature Act of 1873 did was to ensure that if there were ever a conflict between common law and equity, the latter would prevail. The modern legislation embodying this effect is to be found in the Supreme Court Act 1981 s.49(1) (later renamed Senior Courts Act, again to avoid any confusion following the creation of the Supreme Court of the United Kingdom):

"Subject to the provisions of this or any other Act, concurrent every Court exercising jurisdiction in England or Wales in any administration civil cause or matter shall continue to administer law and equity of law on the basis that, <u>wherever there is any conflict or variance between the rules of equity and the rules of the common law with reference to the same matter, the rules of equity shall prevail</u>"

In a way, this was a return to the medieval relationship when equity was a corrective and conscientious force within the common law courts; but faced again with a mono-jurisdictional court, equity is now the overriding and corrective principle, with all the force of statute rather than convention or understanding. The existence of a beneficial interest which takes priority over a legal title, previously only recognised in the law of equity or conscience, is now central to the law. There is now one jurisdiction in one court; but there are clearly two principles – there must be, otherwise one would not be able to take priority over another as per the statute.

As far as the tax courts are concerned, it is the Chancery Division which has jurisdiction; indeed, it is within the High Court's Chancery Division that the UT sits. All the principles of equity and beneficial ownership were bred and nurtured within the equity courts, transferred into the Chancery Division and are therefore inherent within the tax courts by virtue of the 1873 Act and the 1981 equivalent, then sealed with the 2009 tribunal reforms.

---

[1] Robert Lowe, Viscount Sherbrooke (1811-92) in a speech reported in Hansard 11 April 1870, col. 1639

As far as collecting taxes is concerned, HMRC has responsibility for doing this based on assessment of taxes based upon legislation; but upon whom is the tax assessed? Who actually owns the capital asset which produces the income? This is the key question. As far as IHT and CGT (the capital taxes) are concerned, the value and gain respectively will be taxed upon the beneficial owner i.e. the person that ultimately owns it, as per the centuries-old equitable principles enforced by the 1981 Act.

But before the capital taxes, how is beneficial ownership reflected through income tax laws?

8.1   Income tax

This part will be split, again, broadly following the division of the states – executive, legislature and judiciary: firstly, looking at how HMRC regard and recognise beneficial ownership through equitable principles and their compliance process; secondly how the tax legislation recognises such principles; and finally, how the courts have done so.

8.1.1   HMRC's recognition of equitable principles

In analysing HMRC's approach to the law and the process of collecting tax, the public has access to HMRC's thought process and their attitude and interpretation of the law, as well as their approach to procedure, within their Manuals which are compiled for the benefit of their staff. As HMRC make clear, these manuals do not provide definitive answers to every case, but certainly from a practitioner's perspective they provide a valuable insight and useful tool.

8.1.1.1   What is HMRC's view on trusts?

Before looking at specific taxes, we should consider a good example of 'pure equity' in action as reflected in HMRC's attitude towards bare trusts. These are trusts whereby the beneficiary has an absolute right to the income and capital; whilst the legal ownership would be enforceable by common law, HMRC do not regard the legal owner as the actual owner. The equitable owner is the real owner as far as HMRC is concerned.[2]

Following the earlier exploration of resulting trusts which would be implied by the courts where two people contribute to the price of a house bought in one person's name, HMRC's approach to that situation with married couples/civil partners and the marital home would be that the legal owner of the house would be holding it as 'bare' trustee, rather than 'resulting'

---

[2]HMRC Guidance CG34320 and TSEM1563

trustee[3]. Bare trusts equate to implied trusts as far as HMRC are concerned. HMRC seem to regard the beneficial interest within the resulting trust scenario as being primarily a non-tax matter, but a legal matter concerning rights of ownership. However, some of HMRC's examples on resulting trusts concern land and buildings[4] as investments rather than as someone's main residence. Whether it is a bare trustee or resulting trustee, the outcome is still the same as far as HMRC are concerned. We could argue that implied (resulting or constructive) trustees are merely types of bare trustee or nominees anyway – having a custodian-like responsibility thrust upon them with no specific terms unlike those of an express trustee. It brings us back to the familiar academic argument about the varying circumstances in which the different types of trusteeship are imposed – whether a remedy to unjust enrichment or a reneged promise or carrying out the presumed intentions of the parties.

As well as resulting trusts, HMRC have their guidance on constructive trusts in the context of CGT and a PPR claim (see below). Their guidance[5] speaks of common-intention constructive trusts in light of proprietary estoppel with common intention, promises, detriment[6] etc. With specific reference to the estoppels, HMRC Guidance states:

"The doctrine of proprietary estoppel is very similar to that of constructive trusts. It applies if the legal owner of the property has encouraged another to believe that they will acquire an interest in the property and that other person has acted to their detriment in reliance on that believe. The Courts will act to prevent unconscionable conduct by the legal owner".[7]

HMRC's view therefore seems to follow the conventional *Gissing v. Gissing* approach of such a trust's being a remedy against an equitable wrong. However, they also point out that a constructive trust and proprietary estoppel are two different things – a monetary award may be made under proprietary estoppel whereas an actual stake in the property in question via a life interest would be needed for a PPR claim by the trustees.[8]

---

[3] HMRC Guidance CG65310

[4] HMRC Guidance TSEM9620

[5] HMRC Guidance CG65420-30

[6] Though the Supreme Court in *Guest v Guest* [2022] UKSC 27 held that full performance of expectation, rather than detriment, was the correct approach when considering the remedy

[7] HMRC Guidance CG65430

[8] HMRC Guidance CG65430

8.1.1.2   Investment income – interest

HMRC's view on interest arising and on whom it is taxed, follows the above analysis – it is taxable on the person who is beneficially receiving or entitled to it:

> "Generally, the person liable to tax will be the person who is entitled to the interest - the <u>beneficial owner</u> of the interest-bearing account or other source of interest".[9]

If there is only one legal and actual (i.e. beneficial) owner of the bank account, there shouldn't be any issue. As with real property, the issue arises when a second potential account holder emerges. When should HMRC tax that second person as a joint account holder? The answer is when that second person also holds a beneficial interest in the underlying interest-bearing capital[10] even if the stake was a gift.

8.1.1.3   Investment income – dividends

HMRC's view of stock or scrip dividends (i.e. dividends paid in the form of more shares) follows that of savings: it is taxable on the person who is beneficially entitled to it.[11] Their guidance states that this could obviously include the legal owner, but could also include beneficial owners as well as bare trust beneficiaries and those with interests in possession i.e. those beneficial owners under a formal trust structure.[12]

Ordinary dividends are taxed in the hands of:

> "any person to whom any distribution is made or treated as made, or the person receiving or entitled to the distribution".[13]

Unlike with stock dividends, HMRC make no mention of beneficial ownership of ordinary dividends. Their guidance merely mirrors the legislation (see below) but focuses further on the definition of what 'paid' means, of when a dividend is paid and the various circumstances in which the rules are applicable in light of the wide definition of a 'distribution'.

8.1.1.4   Investment income – rental income

As seen below, under 'legislation' heading, the main concern with rental income is the person who runs the rental business. HMRC will never regard

---

[9]HMRC Guidance SAIM2400

[10]HMRC Guidance SAIM2420

[11]HMRC Guidance SAIM5160

[12]Ibid

[13]HMRC Guidance SAIM5020

rental income as a 'trade'[14], but they often do recognize rental as a 'business'[15] and so who runs that business is the main criterion as to who is entitled to receive the rent, which could be a formal trustee (HMRC discuss the position of an IIP trust),[16] a partnership or even a letting agent.[17] Property income does not come under the heading of savings or investments as far as HMRC's guidance is concerned. However, it will not be regarded as earned income either – it would come under the old Schedule A (abolished in 2005 for individuals) whereas earned income comes under the old Schedules DI and DII (trade, profession and vocations) and Schedule E (employment income). Schedules D and E were abolished in 2005 and 2003 respectively.

There are some exceptions (or special rules) to this, recognised by HMRC,[18] and to which equitable principles apply. The first is joint ownership (outside a partnership scenario) by married parties – see below about Form 17. The second is property owned by a partnership. As discussed above, a partnership is a lot like a bare trust in that the partners are the beneficial owners and may not be the same as the legal owners. For all tax purposes the partnership itself is transparent and the partners are taxed on their share of the profits based on their beneficial share in the partnership property. If the rental property is a partnership asset, then the profits/losses will follow the beneficial partnership share and not the legal ownership.

8.1.2 How does equity feature in the tax compliance process?

In this section, we take a brief look at forms, not only compliance forms concerning self-assessment but also Companies Act matters concerning declaration of ownership of companies and the trust registration service.

With self-assessment, an example of HMRC's approach to equity and beneficial interests through a resulting trust (a common intention resulting trust) can be found on Form IHT404 as part of IHT compliance. This form is used as part of a deceased's (UK-domicile and non-excepted) estate return (IHT400) to record assets that were owned jointly with another person at the

---

[14]E.g. *Salisbury House v. Fry* (1930) 15 TC 266 (HL)

[15]For IHT purposes, Business Property Relief may be available if a property is not "wholly or mainly one of…. making or holding investments" under s.105(3) IHTA 1984. Following the *Elizabeth Ramsey* (2013) case, concerning s.162 incorporation relief for CGT, HMRC will generally call a rental property a business for s.162 purposes if more than 20 hours a day are spent on it, per HMRC Guidance CG65715

[16]HMRC Guidance PIM1045

[17]HMRC Guidance PIM1020

[18]HMRC Guidance PIM1030

time of death. HMRC will want to know whether the deceased was entitled to the (default) 50% share, or whether their contribution warrants a lesser or greater assessment; or the deceased may have beneficially owned 100% of the asset – the joint owner's name merely being added as a legal owner despite their not beneficially owning any of it i.e. a classic resulting trust scenario, with the joint legal owners holding the asset on trust for the sole (deceased) beneficial owner. A section within the instructions of the form reads:

> "Sometimes assets may be owned jointly with another person, but one person provided all the money, either in an account or to buy an asset. For example, an elderly person who has difficulty getting out, may add the name of a relative to an account for convenience so the relative may draw out money on the elderly person's behalf. If the person who provided all the money dies, then their share of this account will be the whole".

This last sentence again echoes Eyre CB's statement in *Dyer v. Dyer* in 1788 about the person who advances the money owning the estate.

Form 17 is another form which reflects HMRC's approach to beneficial ownership. Indeed, the form is effectively HMRC's own deed as it records beneficial ownership of jointly owned property between married couples or civil partners. A common example of this being completed is when rental income is to be split in another proportion from the default 50:50. However, because the beneficial ownership ratio is being split for tax purposes then HMRC must be sure that under equitable law the beneficial ownership reflects that demand – an actual trust deed must be attached to the form because a trust is being created – the 50:50 legal ownership is different from the beneficial ownership and the taxpayer wants the income tax to follow that beneficial ownership, not the legal ownership.

As far as limited companies are concerned, from June 2016 private UK limited companies and LLPs have had to declare those who are the PSC i.e. those who have significant control, which is beneficial ownership of 25%+ of the entity (or 25% of the voting rights). The old Annual Returns (AR01s), which gave details of legal shareholders, are now called 'Confirmation Statements' which consist of the PSC register along with other company details including shareholdings, trade and officers' details as before which must still be filed annually to Companies House and are available to the public.

Companies are therefore exposed to the equitable concept of beneficial ownership too – no longer is the pure legal ownership of the shares of any relevance, it is who actually owns them i.e. who has the beneficial ownership.

Trusts themselves, the ultimate progeny of equity, are now subject to the same registration of beneficial ownership through the Trust Registration Service (TRS). The EU's 4AMD became law in the UK on 26 June 2017 when the Money Laundering, Terrorist Financing and Transfer of Funds (Information on the Payer) Regulations SI 2017/692 came into force. This required that all UK express trusts (i.e. those deliberated created by a settlor) or non-UK trusts with UK lex situs assets which were subject to any UK tax charge had to register. This criterion for registration of the trust's being deliberately created means that all implied trusts are excluded from the process.

The concept of reporting the existence of a trust was not entirely new as HMRC were required to know about it for income tax/CGT purposes and would issue a tax return (SA900). However, the old paper Form 41-G, whilst asking about the settlor, the trustees and the initial settled assets, did not ask anything about the beneficiaries, and that is what is revolutionary about TRS. All actual and potential beneficiaries must be declared to the TRS, even if it is just a class of beneficiaries. Someone who has actually received a benefit from a trust would need to have been reported to HMRC anyway via the trust's income tax return as it would affect a discretionary trust's tax pool in relation to the 45% refundable tax credit which the beneficiary has received. The beneficiaries would generally report themselves to HMRC to use the tax credit. All of that is nothing new; but the need to disclose details of a potential beneficiary, even if only the class has been identified, is new. Trustees must now disclose the names, date of birth, National Insurance details, an address and passport number (alternatively a national ID number for non-UK residents) for all actual beneficiaries.

5AMLD came into force in June 2018 and EU-member states were required to bring it into domestic law by 20 January 2020. In the UK this will require the same type of trusts to report to the TRS even if they have no UK tax liability. Not only that, but any non-EU trust which has a business relationship with an 'obliged entity' in the UK (e.g. lawyers, accountants, banks) would also be so obliged. There is still some uncertainty about the precise details, but concern has arisen about subsequent access to the trust register. Currently only HMRC and certain law enforcement agencies have access to the register. The current proposal, however, is to allow access to anyone who claims to have a 'legitimate interest'. This should deny speculative viewings but there are concerns surrounding vulnerable people and minors whose identities should remain out of the public gaze.

This is, arguably, as significant as the PSCs for limited companies insofar as it gives official recognition to the concept of beneficial owners. Obviously, a trust is a trust precisely because the legal and beneficial ownership has been split; with limited companies the legal and beneficial ownerships of the company are generally fused. An argument in favour of the TRS is that the government will not necessarily know that the legal and beneficial ownerships in a property have been split; there is no requirement to submit a trust deed and (aside from reporting an income tax/CGT liability) no requirement to tell the government or HMRC that the legal owner of the property (which they will know about) is not actually the real and beneficial owner. Whilst the legal owner of the property might be recorded as such on the Land Registry, there is nothing to say whether there is any other beneficial owner if there is only one legal owner.[19] There is presumption in favour of beneficial ownership being the same as legal ownership,[20] but nothing to confirm split ownership nor in whom that beneficial ownership lies. By bringing in the TRS the government is arguably bringing trust compliance in line with that for limited companies and ensuring that transparency is applied uniformly, or near uniformly. The public has access to the Companies House register, whereas at the moment they do not have access to the TRS.

8.1.3   How legislation reflects equitable principles

HMRC's guidance is not law, but it is their interpretation of the legislation (and indeed case law) and indicates how they might (or might not) respond in various circumstances in reality. HMRC's attitude to ownership follows equitable law. However, in comparison to HMRC guidance, the legislation is the source of common law cases – the source of law, rather than equity with which it might be in conflict.

8.1.3.1   Investment income – interest

Under ITTOIA 2005 s.371, for interest received:

> "The person liable for any tax charged under this Chapter is the person receiving or entitled to the interest"

As with CGT, there is no reference to any legal or beneficial owner, the legislation concerns itself with actual receipt or entitlement to the interest

---

[19]The TR1 Form has a tick box when ownership is transferred to more than one owner (maximum of four) and asks whether the land will be held in joint-ownership, tenants-in-common or in trust. If the latter, it counts as a declaration of trust

[20]Per *Stack v. Dowden* [2007] 2 AC 432 (HL)

and reliance is placed upon HMRC's guidance to define the beneficial owner. The words *receiving or entitled* reflect the historic income tax legislation and leaves the question open about whether this means the legal or beneficial owner.

8.1.3.2 Investment income – dividends

For the receipt of UK company dividends under ITTOIA 2005 s.385, the tax burden falls upon:

> *"the person receiving or entitled to the distribution".*

This mirrors the historic interest legislation cited above with no reference to legal or beneficial owners.

UK-source dividend income is taxed on a 'paid' rather than 'arising' basis as it is for interest, stock dividends and non-UK dividend income.

However, s.410 of the same Act concerning stock dividends and states:

> *"If an individual is <u>beneficially entitled</u> to that share capital, income is treated as arising to the individual"*

8.1.3.3 Investment income – rental income

ITTOIA 2005 s.271 states that the person liable for profits of a property business is:

> *"the person receiving or entitled to the profits"*

So once again we see the expression 'entitled to receive', with no reference to legal or beneficial owners. In this instance, the importance revolves around who is running the property business.[21] This is different from someone owning a purely passive investment and collecting dividends or interest. Therefore, mere beneficial ownership is less important; instead, the business structure is the main issue.

Investment income law has always been drafted quite widely. As far back as the Income Tax Act 1918, the phrase 'receiving or entitled to receive' applied to the receipt of interest and dividends under Schedule D of that Act and the words survive today. This phrase keeps the ownership open to either legal or beneficial ownership – the legal owner actually receiving the income, but the beneficial owner being the one entitled. It is only through the courts, HMRC's interpretation and the 1981 Act that beneficial ownership has become the pre-eminent form over legal.

---

[21]HMRC Guidance PIM1020

8.1.3.4   *Transfer of Assets Abroad*

Current legislation governing the TOAA is found within ITA 2007 ss.720-751. This applies when a UK-resident individual transfers an asset abroad and, as a result of that transfer (or any 'associated operation'), income becomes payable to an offshore person/entity with the UK transferor/vendor (or spouse or civil partner) continuing to enjoy that income or the asset. An income tax charge is then imposed (based upon the 'relevant income' or the value of the asset) upon the UK individual if the various conditions are met.[22] This is effectively a settlor-interested trust being imposed with the settlor being treated as the true beneficial owner of the asset who never successfully disposed of it. For income arising after 10 March 1981,[23] the TOAA legislation can extend even further, with someone in the UK benefiting from the transfer, but who was not the transferor, potentially being taxed on that income.

In many respects the TOAA legislation is another excellent example of a pure trust situation being recognised within the tax legislation (more specifically, the anti-avoidance chapter within ITA 2007). This is by no means a new piece of legislation. It can trace its lineage back to s.100 Income Tax Act 1842 (so 80 years older than the settlements legislation). The Finance Acts 1936 and 1938 (sections 18 and 28 respectively) contained the source of the modern legislation, with the Income Tax Act 1952 (section 412) then being carried over into and ICTA 1970 s.478 and ICTA 1988 s.739 respectively, before finally settling within ITA 2007. Whilst older than the settlements legislation, the two pieces of legislation are certainly close relatives in that an asset has legally been passed to others who must hold it on trust for the original recipients who, in turn, retain the beneficial interest as they never successfully gave it away. This trust is being imposed by the legislation against the wishes of the parties who wish the actual recipient to be the new owner in every respect. However, to counter this an implied settlor-interested trust is employed to ensure the beneficial ownership stays with the original owner (who is now the settlor), and who is taxed accordingly.

If the trusts borne out of the TOAA and settlements legislation had to be categorised it would most likely be in the mould of a traditional constructive trust. There has been no breach of law, no fraud or abuse of fiduciary

---

[22]This individual could even potentially be caught by the legislation as a 'quasi-transferor' if their limited company makes the transfer (*HMRC v. Fisher* [2021] EWCA Civ 1438)

[23]ITA 2007 s.731, introduced by s.45 Finance Act 1981, following the House of Lords decision in *Vestey v. IR Commrs* [1980] AC 1148, which held that only the transferor or their spouse could be chargeable under the existing legislation

position of responsibility, but in HMRC's mind there has been a wrong of sorts. Tax avoidance, unlike evasion, is perfectly legal and there is the old quote which sums up the attitude which HMRC has been trying to combat for some years:

> "No man in the country is under the smallest obligation, moral or other, so to arrange his legal relations to his business or property as to enable the Inland Revenue to put the largest possible shovel in his stores. The Inland Revenue is not slow, and quite rightly, to take every advantage which is open to it under the Taxing Statutes for the purposes of depleting the taxpayer's pocket. And the taxpayer is in like manner entitled to be astute to prevent, so far as he honestly can, the depletion of his means by the Inland Revenue"[24]

Thus, if the transfer is for genuine commercial reasons and/or

> "it would not be reasonable to draw the conclusion, from all the circumstances of the case, that the purpose of avoiding liability to taxation was the purpose, or one of the purposes, for which the relevant transactions or any of them were effected"[25]

no wrong would have been committed. There is no malevolent intent, so neither equity nor legislation will impose constructive trusteeship. This 'motive defence' within TOAA, is something which is missing from the settlements legislation. TOAA is another example of HMRC expressly recognising a trust's being imposed to solve a perceived wrong being committed, but at least allows for commercial transfers. The settlements legislation, as we have seen, requires some intention to avoid tax but there is no specific, statutory, motive-based exemption as there is with TOAA.

8.1.4   The Courts

This section pulls together the legislation and HMRC's guidance and analyses how the courts (including the tax tribunals, the old General and Special Commissioners and their modern equivalents, the FTT and UT respectively) have recognised and interpreted those equitable principles via an implied trust for income tax purposes over the years. Here we look at the manifestation of the government and HMRC's approach to equitable principles within the courts.

---

[24]Per Lord Clyde, *Ayrshire Pullman Motor Services v. Inland Revenue* [1929] 14 TC 754, at 763,764
[25]ITA 2007 s.737

8.1.4.1   Investment income – interest

A common example of when an implied trust might be imposed is when joint names are added to a bank account to ascertain the ownership of the capital and the resulting interest.

The case of *Aroso v. Coutts & Co*[26] is a good example of when there was a joint bank account in law but the argument by IR was that there was only one beneficial owner, that the gift of the account to the co-owner was effectively incomplete and a resulting trust was the outcome. In that case, the Chancery Division of the High Court actually decided that there was sufficient evidence to show that the original account holder did intend to make a gift of half of the account – thus reflecting the legal position. As with resulting trusts and ascertaining the presumed intention, all circumstances will be looked into by the courts; as well as deciding whether a solely owned asset was intended to be owned by both parties, so too a jointly owned asset should be examined closely to establish whether it was intended as a gift.

In the *Aroso* case, Collins J pointed out the long-standing position that a resulting trust would be the default starting position with a transfer (as this is not land), therefore the circumstances would need to be looked into as to whether that presumption should be rebutted in favour of a gift. The appellant in that case argued that there was no intention of a gift and that he was named joint account holder for convenience purposes only; however, the defendant bank insisted that the original account holder knew what he was doing and intended to give the joint holder a beneficial interest. The presumption of a resulting trust is easily rebutted; the bank succeeding in doing so and the court held that a gift had been made. If no contribution to the account or withdrawal had been made or even if the other owner did not know about it, then one might think in the first instance that that other owner was merely acting as a trustee for the other person; but Collins J pointed out that those circumstances would not rule out beneficial ownership too if other circumstances pointed in that direction.

Another, earlier, example along similar lines which also appeared in the Chancery Division was the case of *Young v Sealey*.[27] In that case too, money and shares were deposited by one person but into a joint bank account (an aunt and nephew in this case). The nephew never paid any money in nor took any out. Upon the aunt's death, her personal representatives (the plaintiffs) claimed that the nephew was merely a joint trustee with the sole

---

[26][2002] 1 All ER 241 (Ch D)

[27][1949] 1 All ER 92 (Ch D)

IMPLIED TRUSTS

beneficial interest lying with the aunt. However, evidence was put forward showing that the aunt had intended it to be a gift - that the funds should be for the nephew's benefit too and that he should have whatever was in the account upon his aunt's death. The plaintiffs argued that as the gift was effectively posthumous (i.e. postponed until after aunt's death) and not in accordance with the terms of the Wills Act 1837, then it could not be a testamentary gift. However, Romer J would not allow that technicality to defeat the nephew's claim to the money and shares.

8.1.4.2   Investment income – dividends

The discretionary nature of dividends often means that they can be over/under-declared, and as such, the danger of the settlements legislation being applied is greater than it is with earned income and interest.

One of the main authorities, *Vandervell* (which went before the House of Lords twice) discussed resulting trusts concerning the receipt of dividends. Another, more recent case which appeared before the FTT also discussed receipt of dividends and the settlements legislation; however, the *Patmore* case employed a constructive trust.

Example 1: Vandervell cases
Vandervell consisted of three cases. The first was a tax case on which we shall focus exclusively here. The second case is not directly relevant to this discussion. The third case concerned the status of company shares in a death estate which we shall look at briefly in the IHT sub-section below.

Guy Anthony Vandervell was a wealthy businessman who wished to endow the Royal College of Surgeons to found a chair in Pharmacology. In 1958, a donation of £150,000 (which took the form of 100,000 shares in his family's company) was made to the College which would then receive the intended £150,000 in dividends (£245,000 of dividends was eventually paid out). As a charity, the College would not be subject to income tax on those dividends. However, as part of the arrangement the College was required to grant an option to Mr Vandervell's family trust (actually a limited company called Vandervell Trustees Ltd – 'the company') to buy the shares back in the future for £5,000 (which they did in November 1961). In January 1965, Mr Vandervell executed a deed transferring any remaining interest in the shares to the company. He died in March 1967.

The first case[28] concerned the settlements legislation and revolved around the dividends paid to the College, which IR believed (until the deed of 1965)

---

[28][1967] 2 AC 291 (HL)

should actually have been taxed upon Mr Vandervell as settlor of a settlement under Income Tax Act 1952 s.404. Alternatively, IR argued, he had failed to divest himself of the shares under s.415 of that Act. The House of Lords agreed with IR's submissions – but only by a majority. Lord Upjohn gave the majority verdict and reminded the court that:

> "Where A transfers, or directs a trustee for him to transfer, the legal estate in property to B otherwise than for valuable consideration it is a question of the intention of A in making the transfer whether B was to take beneficially or on trust and, if the latter, on what trusts. If, as a matter of construction of the document transferring the legal estate, it is possible to discern A's intentions, that is an end of the matter and no extraneous evidence is admissible to correct and qualify his intentions so ascertained.

> But if, as in this case (a common form share transfer), the document is silent, then there is said to arise a resulting trust in favour of A. But this is only a presumption and is easily rebutted. All the relevant facts and circumstances can be considered in order to ascertain A's intentions with a view to rebutting this presumption"[29]

The issue in this case was the option itself. The question was whether it was held by the company absolutely, or effectively retained by Mr Vandervell. Lord Upjohn cited Plowman J in the High Court who said:

> "As I see it, a man does not cease to own property simply by saying 'I don't want it'. If he tries to give it away the question must always be: has he succeeded in doing so or not?[30]"

Lord Upjohn applied this question to the option when it was granted by the College to the company and decided:

> "(it) was a matter of courtesy; at this time the college had no legal or beneficial interest in the shares and they could only comply with it. They did so in due course and in fact were not in the least degree interested in the ultimate fate of the shares after they had received the promised dividends. But in law I cannot doubt that it was the appellant acting by his agent, Mr. Robins, who procured the college to grant the option to the trustee company"

Lord Upjohn therefore concluded that:

---

[29][1967] 2 AC 291 at 314
[30][1966] Ch 261 at 275

IMPLIED TRUSTS

"the intention was that the trustee company should hold on such trusts as might thereafter be declared by the trustee company or the appellant (Mr Vandervell) and so in the event for the appellant."

The majority verdict was that because there was no evidence that the company was the beneficial owner of the option, it was subject to a resulting trust in favour of Mr Vandervell; and he should be subject to the surtax charge on the dividends. Even if it had been the intention to create an express trust in favour of the company, the terms of such a trust were not clear meaning the formalities for an express trust had not been met. With the failure of an express trust this would have led to the imposition of a resulting trust anyway (an 'automatic' resulting trust in that case). Indeed, Edwin Simpson[31] highlights the significance of this judgement and takes issue with a sentence uttered by Lord Upjohn:

"the presumption of a resulting trust is no more than a long stop to provide the answer when the relevant facts and circumstances fail to yield a solution"

Simpson points out there are two 'long stops' in this case: the first presents itself when it cannot be determined whether a gift or transfer to a trust was intended; and second when there was an intention to create a trust *"but where further details of the disposition are ineffective or unknown"*. These two backstops represent, effectively, both types of resulting trusts: that of 'common-intention' and the other of 'automatic' respectively. In the third Vandervell case (*Re Vandervell (No. 3)*),[32] this was the same as the interpretation made by Megarry J and is of significance to the earlier discussion regarding the difference between the two types of resulting trust.

This is an interesting case because not one, but two Law Lords dissented.[33] Lords Donovan and Reid held there was every intention for the option to be held by the company beneficially and thus Mr Vandervell had divested himself of the underlying shares. They were unable to link the granting of the option as any condition to the ultimate gift of the shares to the College; they also considered that the option originated from the company, not Mr Vandervell personally. It went to show that even at the very highest levels,

---

[31] *Restitution & Equity* Vol 1 pages 9-10

[32] [1974] Ch 269

[33] The House of Lords was unanimous in its verdict that Law of Property Act 1925 s.53 was not in issue here as the beneficiary directed the legal owner (i.e. the bank holding the shares) to transfer the legal ownership. This meant the legal and beneficial ownership were dealt with together whereas s.53 concerns itself solely with beneficial ownership

the matter was not clear cut and divisions surrounding the imposition and status of implied trusts exist even in the highest court in the land.

Example 2: Patmore v. HMRC

The case of *David Patmore*[34] is a fairly typical settlements legislation case (one in which a company was owned by a husband and wife); but it is also unusual because of the conclusion which the judge reached concerning constructive trusts.

The facts of Patmore were a little unusual too, which may be why a constructive trust, rather than a simple settlor-interested trust under the settlements legislation, was imposed. Whilst this ultimately became a solely husband and wife company, it started out as one owned by another family. It was then bought out by Mr and Mrs Patmore, with Mr Patmore holding 98% of the shares and being sole director. Prior to the sale he had already owned 15 out of 100 issued shares. After the sale, Mrs Patmore held the remaining 2% of the shares and became company secretary. The total purchase price of the shares was £320,000, paid for with an initial £100,000 payment coming from re-mortgaging the joint home. However, the remaining £220,000 was outstanding as a debt to be paid off in instalments over the next year solely by Mr Patmore. Shortly after the sale, the company's original 100 shares were re-named 'A' shares and 100 new shares, with no voting rights, were created - these were 'B' shares, 10 of which were transferred to Mrs Patmore. Around £20,000 of dividends were paid on the B shares, but Mrs Patmore gave all her B share dividends to her husband who used the money to pay off the purchase debt.

The Patmores argued that this occurred because Mrs Patmore's 2% holding would have protected her from the acquisition risks but still allowed her to receive a fair share of dividends. The plan had been for the B share dividends to pay off both the outstanding loan and mortgage, but as profits were not as high as they had hoped, the priority was to pay off the loan. HMRC did not accept this reasoning when seeking to impose the settlement legislation under ICTA 1988 s.660A(1) (as it was then). Mr Patmore's tax returns for 1999/2000 to 2002/03 inclusive were therefore amended to include his wife's dividends. HMRC's argument was that the B shares were 'settled' upon Mrs Patmore and that Mr Patmore had used his control of the company to settle a disproportionate amount of dividends upon his wife was who was paying income tax at a lower rate – a classic settlements scenario. HMRC said that there had been no need to create the B shares – they carried no special

---

[34]TC00619 (2010, FTT)

IMPLIED TRUSTS

dividend rights, it was all part of an arrangement to divert the dividends to Mrs Patmore.

However, the FTT dismissed HMRC's argument under the settlements legislation and allowed Mr Patmore's appeal. Whilst there was undoubtedly an 'arrangement', there was no gift wholly of income so the spousal statutory exemption would have applied, thus allowing such an arrangement whereby both parties owned shares. But that aside, the FTT also found that there was no element of bounty within the arrangement – a key ingredient with the settlements legislation. Mrs Patmore was jointly liable for the purchase debt and the house mortgage; she had contributed equally to the purchase of the shares but only received two of the 42.5 A shares to which she was entitled (in addition to 10 B shares). Far from benefitting from the arrangement, as normally happens in a settlements arrangement, she was worse off. Indeed, so worse off that she was actually the victim of an equitable wrong. Whilst FTT refused to impose the settlements legalisation's settlor-interested trust, they instead imposed a constructive trust upon Mr Patmore with Mrs Patmore having sole beneficial ownership over her remaining 40.5 A shares. The court's view was that whilst there was no commercial justification for the arrangement, neither was it gratuitous – rather an insufficient and inadequate recognition of Mrs Patmore's rights in the company.

This was the unusual aspect: neither party had mentioned constructive trusts anywhere in their submissions and no authorities were cited concerning trusts or even equitable principles. The judge applied the remedy on her own initiative on the basis that:

"…Mrs Patmore was entitled to half of the 85 'A' shares but in fact received only two 'A' shares and the promise of almost valueless 'B' shares"

And that:

"Either she (Mrs Patmore) intended to give up her entitlement in favour of her husband or she did not. I have found as a matter of fact that she did not intend a gift. This led me to conclude that Mr Patmore held some of the shares on constructive trust for her and that her receipt of the B shares and dividends up to 42.5% of the dividend paid did not therefore involve an element of bounty on his part"

Clearly, therefore, the judge saw a wrong and righted it with a constructive trust. There was no discussion as to what type of constructive trust it was (i.e. 'common-intention' as per HMRC's guidance, or a 'traditional' one). Not that it is of any great importance, certainly from a practical perspective, but it could be either. One could argue it is similar to an unlawful dividend being declared. However, considering the use of the judge's language i.e. Mrs Patmore's not having 'fair recognition' of her investment, along with talk of the investment's being in a joint venture and her not intending a gift of her entitlement (as quoted above); this all resonates with the components of a common-intention constructive trust rather than arising as an operation of law.

The husband and wife element of this is interesting too. This was discussed above, but the judge in *Patmore* made reference to the old aggregation of marital tax assessment when justifying why the spousal exemption for applied shares, but not dividends (i.e. gifts wholly and substantially of income):

> "... this is because Parliament wished to allow a person to entirely divest themselves of property in favour of their spouse in that for all purposes separate taxation would then apply. What Parliament did not want is for a spouse to decide year on year that his or her income could be given to the spouse in order to get lower tax rates".[35]

This unilateral imposition of a constructive trust is very relevant. The FTT, a first-instance administrative court, imposed a chancery court remedy, and did so with no persuasion or dissuasion from the parties' representatives, using only its inherent equitable jurisdiction.

An article in the *Trust and Estate Law & Tax Journal*[36] by Adam Craggs[37] gives a good outline of the case. He too points out the unusual nature of the judge's imposing a constructive trust – that it was not raised by the parties and that the judge imposed one at all. He suggests that had the FTT simply found that the element of bounty was not there and dismissed the appeal, that would not have been unusual; but this surprising initiative taken by the judge was.

Toward the end of his article, Craggs turns to the general nature of constructive trusts, highlighting their flexible and remedial nature. Indeed, after citing Edmund Davies LJ in *Carl Zeiss Stiftung* (cited above), he comments that they may be too flexible:

> "Constructive trusts have been found to exist in a series of disparate and changing situations. However there is a danger that constructive trusts may become too flexible and, in the words of Lord Denning in his judgment in

---

[35] At page 75

[36] January/February 2011

[37] Solicitor and partner at the tax disputes resolution team at Reynolds Porter Chamberlain LLP

IMPLIED TRUSTS

Hussey v. Palmer ([1972] 1 WLR 1338), become employed 'whether justice and good conscience require it'. Such use of constructive trusts can fairly be regarded as an approach can achieve justice in an individual case it is often at the expense of certainty".

And, most damningly,

"The Patmore decision has introduced further uncertainty in this important area of law".

The title to his article, "*A Step Too Far*", gives us a clue as to the gist of his opinion of the case. To a large extent he is right. The settlements legislation has, for a very long time, been the main concern with arrangements like this. The *Arctic Systems* case was more of a milestone case with husband and wife companies and dividends; but that was addressing settlements legislation only. It was not raising any points specifically about implied trusts. Over the decades, when it has come to share transactions, tax practitioners have needed to consider other matters such as Transactions in Securities rules (first introduced in 1960) and potentially those concerning Employment-Related Securities. The imposition of constructive trusts on a court's whim is indeed now another factor to consider when undertaking tax planning; it is particularly difficult when the flexibility of these trusts and the court's discretion over them is such that certainty is compromised.

The article's sub-headline reads:

"Adam Craggs examines the case of Patmore, which extends the application of the constructive trust in tax law"

In the sense that it will give practitioners something else to muse over alongside the settlements legislation, the headline is quite right. As the publication is aimed at practitioners, that is probably all that matters. But looking at this from an historical angle, the sub-heading arguably implies that constructive trusts have had little impact on tax law before. But it has always been there. The FTT simply used its inherent equitable jurisdiction and flexibility to right a wrong.

Craggs also makes an interesting point about Mr Patmore's not being <u>legally</u> represented (i.e. by a lawyer) as an explanation for why the constructive trust point was not made by Mr Patmore, who *"without legal representation was not in a position to comment on it"*. Mr Patmore was represented, but by an accountant, not a wholly unusual occurrence within the FTT; but HMRC was represented by tax counsel. This is another interesting point from a practice perspective. Accountants have not, historically, had to delve into the realms of implied trusts. However, the article was written by a lawyer and in a publication most of whose readers are private-client solicitors.

The argument here is that the ability of the tax courts to apply a constructive trust has always been there, certainly since the Supreme Court Act 1981 and even since the 'fusion' of 1873. Equity prevails over all courts. The FTT is a tax court and *Patmore* could have been appealed to the UT – which is now effectively the Chancery Division of the High Court, which is the modern descendent of the Chancery Court and so on. The case is indeed an excellent example of a tax court (particularly a first instance court) imposing a constructive trust, and it is an early (if not first) example of that happening. From a practitioner's perspective we can see the significance; but from an academic perspective, it is nothing out of the ordinary besides a stark and excellent illustration of equitable principles being inherent and alive in the modern tax courts.

8.1.4.3 Investment income – rental income

As mentioned above, as far rental income is concerned, HMRC have very much formalised their recognition of beneficial ownership, certainly as far as married couples are concerned where a 50:50 holding is presumed, unless a Form 17 and accompanying trust deed allows for a different ratio.

Generally, as stated above with HMRC guidance and legislation, the person taxed on the rental income is the person who runs the business and is therefore entitled to the rent and receives it. That will largely be a question of fact so we will not look at this as it will tell us nothing of equitable ownership – the person who runs the business is the person who receives the rent. Whilst rental income is classed as investment (or unearned) income for many tax purposes, it might as well be treated as earned.

One case from the FTT which illustrates their acknowledgment of equitable principles between joint owners is the case of *Akan*.[38] In this case, the dispute was the assignment of rental income (amongst other things) in the absence of a Form 17.

Mrs Akan was appealing against assessments of income tax issued for the years 1997/98 to 2009/10 and 2011/12. The property in question was owned jointly with her husband and they lived there until 1997 after which time it was let out. In 2006 she and her husband separated, and she was given full title to the property. Their divorce was finalised in October 2011, the tenant at the property was evicted in October 2012 and the property was sold in

---

[38]TC6498 May 2018 (FTT)

IMPLIED TRUSTS

November of that year. HMRC claimed that Mrs Akan should have completed tax returns for the rental income on a 50/50 ownership basis between 1997/98 and 2004/05, with her being accountable for 100% of it for 2008/09 onwards. HMRC pointed out that the default split for income on the jointly owned property before 2006 is 50:50 for married couples unless a Form 17 had been completed removing that presumption; no such Form had been received. Following the issuing of the closure notice on that basis, Mrs Akan issued her appeal on the basis that her husband had always kept the rental income and told her that he was declaring the profits to HMRC. It was a controlling and abusive relationship. The tribunal held that, with respect of the rental income, due to the nature of this relationship her husband was effectively acting as an agent and thus keeping part of the income. In this instance 80% of the profits would be assigned to the husband and only 20% assigned to the appellant for 2006/07 to 2008/09:

> *"We have accepted that Mrs Akan found Mr Gelman controlling and abusive and from that we conclude that she did not voluntarily consent to his retention of the net profits; we have concluded that he managed the property and her acquiescence in that activity made him in our view her agent".*[39]

So even in the absence of a Form 17 and trust deed, the FTT decided that Mrs Akan was acting as agent for her husband who was keeping the rental income. No mention was made of the words 'implied' or 'constructive' trusts within the judgment; indeed, the issue for the FTT was whether Mrs Akan had a 'reasonable excuse' for not declaring them on her tax return. However, they might as well have used the words 'implied trust'. Agency laws are different from the laws of trust – an agent is not a legal owner, merely a representative; but as discussed above with partnerships, it is arguably akin to a bare trust scenario. Mrs Akan was the 100% legal owner after the divorce but because the husband was retaining all the income, they assessed the beneficial ownership to sit 80:20 for husband and wife. Mrs Akan was essentially the trustee. HMRC were perfectly within their rights to assess Mrs Akan on her 50% then 100% share as the beneficial ownership followed that legal ownership in the absence of any trust deed to the contrary. But in the circumstances of their relationship, the FTT felt it would be unconscionable for Mrs Akan to shoulder the legal burden of the rental income. This is pure equity at work, almost subconsciously within the FTT as there was no judicial explanation about the need to exercise the court's inherent equitable jurisdiction and impose a constructive trust in the face of this wrong. There was no formality to point toward any trust or agent

---

[39]Ibid para 37 per Charles Hellier

relationship, they just imposed a nominee arrangement or a bare trust for tax purposes.

8.2 What about capital taxes?

How has the concept of beneficial ownership developed within the two main capital taxes (IHT and CGT) within the executive, judiciary and legislature?

8.2.1 IHT

When assessing the value of someone's estate, HMRC will indeed base their assessment upon beneficial ownership for IHT purposes. The IHT manuals state:

> "The word 'estate' is given its general meaning and includes all property to which the transferor is _beneficially entitled_"[40]

The whole basis of IHT is a charge upon death when the property within one's estate is transferred to his personal representatives or in the diminution of his estate with lifetime gifts. Taking the basic premise of property, it is clearly the beneficial, rather than legal ownership which matters and beneficial ownership means that property "to which a person is entitled, or in which they have an interest for their own benefit".[41]

It is worth pointing out a slight difference in the approaches between the English and Scottish courts. As mentioned in the introduction, whilst IHT is a UK-wide tax, the focus upon beneficial ownership is confined to England, Wales and Northern Ireland. Scotland has a system of unitary ownership unlike England's system whereby a person owning an asset is both a legal and beneficial owner:

> "The inheritance tax charge is concerned with the property to which a person is beneficially entitled. In English law, this includes property which a person owns either legally or beneficially. In Scots law, it is only property that a person owns legally".[42]

The earlier guidance points out that despite an owner of property in England, Wales and Northern Ireland being a legal and beneficial owner, this does not take the focus away ultimately from beneficial ownership, as stated above. A further reminder states that beneficial entitlement does not include ownership "purely in a fiduciary capacity (for example as a trustee) or in

---

[40]HMRC Guidance IHTM04029

[41]HMRC Guidance IHTM04031

[42]HMRC Guidance IHTM04441

a representative capacity (for example as an executor or a trustee in bankruptcy)".[43] In other words, not a bare trust relationship.

But when was beneficial ownership first mentioned in the IHT legislation?

8.2.1.1   IHT Legislation

IHT has transformed a great deal over the years but can trace its lineage back to the Probate Act 1694, whereafter it was contained in the Legacy Duties Act 1796. The idea of a tax upon succession was laid down within Gladstone's Succession Duty Act 1853 within which it was declared in section 33:

> *"every past or future disposition of property by reason whereof any person has or shall become beneficially entitled to any property, or the income thereof, upon the death of any person dying after the time appointed for the commencement of this act, either immediately or after any interval, either certainly or contingently, and either originally or by way of substitutive limitation and every devolution by law of <u>any beneficial interest</u> in property, or the income thereof, upon the death of any person dying after the time appointed for the commencement of this act to any other person in possession or expectancy".*

This was replaced by Estate Duty through the Finance Act 1894 which concerned the deceased's property:

> *"of which the deceased was at the time of his death competent to dispose"*[44]

So, no express mention of beneficial ownership – just the presumption that the deceased was 'competent' to dispose of it, which was defined with s.22(2)a of the 1894 Act:

> *"A person shall be deemed competent to dispose of property if he has such an estate or interest therein"*

The words 'an interest' could potentially mean a beneficial interest as well as a legal one if we presume the intention of the 1853 Act was carried over into the 1894 Estate Duty. After some reforms in 1949 and 1959, this Duty lasted until Capital Transfer Tax was established in its stead by the Finance Act 1975. This tax applied to a deceased's estate, which was defined in s.23(1) of that Act as:

---

[43]HMRC Guidance IHTM04031

[44]FA 1894 s.2(1)a

> *"the aggregate of all the property to which he is <u>beneficially entitled</u>"*

The modern law, as we know it today, is contained within the Inheritance Tax Act 1984, s.5(1) of which reads:

> *"For the purposes of this Act a person's estate is the aggregate of all property to which he is <u>beneficially entitled</u>"*

Therefore, it seems that Estate Duties, Succession Tax and the modern Inheritance Tax have all recognised beneficial ownership as being the bedrock of the law before the income tax legislation. The courts would therefore presumably have little difficulty in imposing a beneficial interest upon a deceased through an implied trust if the facts or the deceased's and another's intention was such. They would not need to call upon their inherent equitable jurisdiction to bestow beneficial ownership – the legislation has already required that beneficial ownership be identified. However, the courts would clearly be needed to ascertain who the beneficial owner is.

Another aspect of interest within IHT legislation is that of 'Gifts with Reservation of Benefit' (GWRB). This occurs, broadly, when A gives away property to B, but continues to benefit from enjoyment or possession of the same property. For IHT purposes that property will remain in the donor's estate for IHT purposes. Finance Act 1986 s.102(3), which concerns GWRB, states:

> *"If, immediately before the death of the donor, there is any property which, in relation to him, is property subject to a reservation then, to the extent that the property would not, apart from this section, form part of the donor's estate immediately before his death, <u>that property shall be treated for the purposes of the 1984 Act as property to which he was beneficially entitled immediately before his death</u>".*

This is arguably a prime example of a resulting trust – an automatic resulting trust if we adopt Lord Diplock's categorisation – as A's gift of the property to B is incomplete, it is *"never drawn off him"*.[45] Indeed, as far as the IHT400 itself is concerned, a GWRB made within seven years of death is treated as any other failed gift which remains in the deceased's estate.[46]

---

[45]Per *Godbold v. Freestone*
[46]Within Form IHT403

IMPLIED TRUSTS

8.2.1.2   IHT and the courts

This subsection discusses the contents of a deceased's estate when considering that, as per IHTA 1984 s.5, it includes those assets to which the deceased was beneficially entitled. That may be some assets which the deceased did own legally but with an additional beneficial co-owner, or indeed did not own legally but owned the beneficial title or a share. The crucial point here is that these assets would be included in a deceased's 'free' estate i.e. those assets which he was deemed to have owned outright and to which he was entitled and which are disposed of by the terms of his will or intestate (as opposed to assets owned under joint tenancy).

Assets included within someone's 'settled' estate would obviously be subject to the rules of equity as 'settled property' within an IIP trust mainly created before March 2006; however, that would not be on account of any implied trust. Settled property is defined[47] as being part of a (systematic) express trust[48] with appointed trustees with a specific mandate e.g. as discretionary trustees or trustees of an IIP trust. We focus on those assets deemed by the courts to be part of a deceased's free estate and treated as if owned outright, rather than being subject to any express trust.

A good example of this is the case of *Aroso v. Coutts & Co*[49] (discussed above).

Another case - *Personal Representatives of Lyon (Dec'd) v. IRC*[50] provides a good example of the GWRB rules as this includes settlement into a discretionary trust. The deceased settled £2.7million in a discretionary trust of which he was one of the beneficiaries along with his children. During his lifetime he only received just under £16,000 and the rest of the trust fund was distributed to his children as per his letter of wishes to the trustees. Upon his death, IR assessed the value of the trust as being in his death estate for IHT purposes on the basis that he was beneficially entitled to the income and capital therein. Finance Act 1986 s.102(1)(b) states that property validly gifted such that it falls out of someone's estate must be bona fide assumed by the donee or that it must be enjoyed to the entire (or virtually entire) exclusion of the donor. IR considered that neither criterion had been met and that the settlement fell outside the deceased's estate. The executors argued

---

[47] IHTA 1984 s.43

[48] However, HMRC guidance IHTM16042 states that the trust can "be imposed by law e.g. intestacy". Arguably this could include a 'traditional' constructive trust but referring to intestacy would indicate imposition by statute rather than the operation of law and the courts.

[49] [2002] 1 All ER 241 (Ch D)

[50] [2007] STC 675

that the deceased's actual receipt of trust assets was insignificant and that IR's approach of deeming that a settlor's having an interest in a discretionary trust would constitute a GWRB was too rigid. However, the Special Commissioner held that to adopt that approach would defeat the entire purpose of GWRB legislation.

The point here is that the gift was incomplete, the recipient hadn't taken complete ownership of the property to the exclusion of the donor – therefore it simply was not a gift and equity will not assume there was a gift even if the intention was such, in which case a trust will be imposed such that the donor retains a beneficial interest. As IHT is all about gifts, the question of whether one has been completed and is a genuine bona fide gift is obviously critical. Two equitable maxims are *"equity will not assist a volunteer"* and *"equity will not perfect an imperfect gift"*;[51] however, in the spirit of good conscience, nor will it *"strive officiously to defeat a gift"*.[52]

Another case of significance is that of *Re Vandervell's Trusts (No. 2)*[53]. The first case was a tax case surrounding the settlements legislation and dividends which we discussed above (hence why this IHT sub-section is included after the one concerning dividends). The second Vandervell case[54] concerned recovery of dividends by the late Mr Vandervell's estate and against company trustees. However, the third case concerned ownership of the underlying shares as part of a death estate.

In the High Court, Megarry J went through the first Vandervell case in some detail and agreed with that judgment that a resulting trust had arisen with Mr Vandervell as the beneficial owner of the shares in question which thus formed part of his death estate. However, the Court of Appeal unanimously reversed that ruling. Lord Denning MR gave his judgment on the basis that by the time of Mr Vandervell's death an express trust had already been created in favour of the company (in January 1965). As Lord Denning pointed out:

"A resulting trust for the settlor is born and dies without any writing at all. It comes into existence whenever there is a gap in the beneficial ownership. It ceases to exist whenever that gap is filled by someone becoming beneficially

---

[51]Both derived from Turner LJ's judgment in *Milroy v. Lord* (1862) 4 De GF&J 264

[52]Per Lord Browne-Wilkinson in *Choithram International SA v. Pagarani* [2001] 1 WLR 1

[53][1974] Ch 269

[54]*Re Vandervell Trustees Ltd* [1971] AC 912

entitled. As soon as the gap is filled by the creation or declaration of a valid trust, the resulting trust comes to an end"[55]

8.2.2 CGT

With CGT the gain is taxable upon the beneficial owner of the asset:

"Capital Gains Tax is charged under TCGA92/S1(1) on the disposal of assets, but it is important to bear in mind that the legal owner of an asset is not necessarily its beneficial owner and that it is beneficial ownership (not legal ownership) which the tax principally follows. The point is particularly important in relation to partnership assets, family and matrimonial or civil partnership property and real property (land) generally"[56]

This guidance is clearer still about the importance of beneficial over legal ownership – with no notion of the owner's being the legal owner as well, nor any reference to Scotland's unitary ownership system. The reference to partnership assets is an important one.

But what does the legislation say?

8.2.2.1 CGT Legislation

The modern legislation (TCGA 1992) makes no mention of beneficial ownership other than with regards to share ownership (just like the historical income tax Acts) and replacement assets upon destruction of the original. Instead, the tax is based predominately on the individual's residence and the nature of the asset being disposed of, rather than the ownership of that asset. This is why HMRC needed to make the position clear in their guidance. The legislation therefore seems to go against the beneficial ownership 'grain', as shown by the legislation's approach to trustees and a very valuable relief.

CGT's most valuable tax relief is PPR. This exempts from CGT, without limit, the profits arising from the sale of a main residence; with the increase in house prices in the UK over the last 20 years or so, realising the value of a house tax-free can be akin to winning the lottery. Married couples and civil partners can only nominate one property to be their principle private residence. However, as we examine below, whereby CGT principles generally focus upon beneficial ownership, like all other areas of tax, when any trust structure is in issue, it is the legal owner who attracts the attention of PPR.

---

[55][1974] Ch 269 at 320

[56]HMRC Guidance CG11700P

PPR exempts from CGT the profits from the disposal of one's main residence, even if it is not reinvested in another property (reliefs such as s.152 TCGA business asset replacement relief for CGT and the 3% surcharge relief from SDLT on second properties all depend on sums' being reinvested). There must be actual physical residence within the property as a permanent main residence (i.e. no signs of temporary or ad hoc living) with the intention for *"permanence, continuity and some expectation of continuity"*[57] from the outset. The CGT exemption applies not only to the period of time occupied but also to the last nine months' ownership irrespective as to whether the owner actually lived there in that final period.[58] There are also further reliefs for other temporary periods of absence as well as for those periods in which the property has been let out. With the increase in property prices over the last 20 years or so, this can yield significant (tax-free) profits. As there are many homeowners in the country, it is the relief probably most widely used outside business and farming circles. Indeed, it is the only relief available under CGT for a purely private residential property. However, whilst the topic of this book is on implied trusts, there is legislation within TCGA concerning settled property and PPR which seemingly turns on its head everything said so far about the primacy of beneficial ownership.

The legislation within TCGA 1992 states that 'settled property' is:

"any property held in trust other than property to which s.60 applies"[59]

Section 60 states that property held by a nominee or bare trust is treated as being owned by the beneficiary absolutely, in accordance with HMRC's well-established view across the tax spectrum of bare trusts. Section 68 defines *"in trust"* to seemingly include *all* (except bare) trusts; it does not address implied trusts specifically at all, even though they are treated the same as bare trusts for tax purposes. Does 'trust' include implied trusts? Or are they to be considered the same as bare trusts for PPR purposes as well? HMRC's guidance comes to our assistance on this point: CG65415 states categorically that assets within an implied trust come within the definition of settled assets for the purposes of s.225.

Whilst the whole theme of this book is about the tax consequences on the beneficiary of an implied trust, TCGA 1992 s.225 is solely concerned with the

---

[57]Taken from *Goodwin v. Curtis* [1998] STC 475 at 478

[58]Before 6 April 2020, that final deemed occupation period was 18 months unless the occupier was disabled and/or in long term residential care and with only one main residence, in which case the period is still 36 months.

[59]Section 68

CGT consequences upon the trustee – the legal owner of the main residence being disposed of. Section 225 states that the *trustees* may receive the benefit of PPR if the residence is occupied by a person entitled to do so under the terms of the settlement. This generally means life tenants with an IIP trust, but HMRC accept that discretionary trust beneficiaries may also come under this heading.[60]

Throughout this book we have seen how the beneficial ownership dictates HMRC's recognition of ownership for taxation purposes, including CGT: the beneficial owner is the focus of the tax burden. In other words, implied trusts are treated in the same manner as bare trusts. However, this relief, the most valuable and widely used of all, bucks that trend. The relief focuses upon the legal owner because of TCGA 1992 s.225.

Section 68 merely states *"any property held in trust"* which s.225 blindly adopts; it lumps implied and express trusts together making the trustee the focus of the relief. Even if an implied trust has been imposed because of an equitable wrong, or a presumed intention under constructive or resulting trusts, the treatment for PPR purposes is the same. The trustees claim the relief, irrespective of whether the trust is express or implied, even though CGT is only assessed on them for the former types of trusts.

Disputes often revolve around whether a trust has been created because this will affect whether the person living in the house can benefit from PPR as occupier, or whether that person is merely the beneficiary and a trustee has been identified as the actual owner but can rely on PPR nonetheless by virtue of that beneficiary. Cases such as *Wagstaff* [61] and *Vincent* [62] looked at whether various arrangements constituted a settlement in the broad sense; *Wagstaff* was a PPR case which argued that a trust had been created and that whilst the taxpayer had never lived in the property sold, the taxpayer trustee could claim PPR as the legal owner. The FTT agreed. (*Vincent* was an IHT case ascertaining whether an IIP had been created for death estate purposes).

HMRC's guidance on the matter of PPR and implied trusts recognises the difference between resulting and constructive trusts[63] and even goes into some detail about common intention constructive trusts looking at cases like

---

[60]Per HMRC Guidance CG65407 citing the case of *Sansom v. Peay* [1976] STC 494

[61]TC3183 January 2014 (FTT)

[62]TC7432 October 2019 (FTT)

[63]HMRC Guidance CG65415

Oxley v Hiscock[64] and *Stack v Dowden*,[65] but only when discussing whether a trust has been created at all – as in the *Wagstaff* case. Indeed, the guidance makes clear that those two cases are non-tax and non-PPR-related. The fact that it is a constructive or resulting trust is thus irrelevant as far as HMRC and the Courts are concerned with s.225; if there is a trust, however created, it is the trustee who can make the relief claim. Whether it is constructive or resulting is purely academic. The only distinction made at all is by asking whether there was an express trust in place[66] – if so, then there clearly cannot be an implied trust.

Either way if there is a trust, then it is settled property. There seems to be academic discussion within HMRC's manuals on the topic of settled property; none of it concerns s.225 or even tax. It is almost as if they are compensating for failing to recognise the beneficiary as being not only the occupier of the property but also the true beneficial owner as well. That beneficial owners should be claiming PPR because under general CGT principles they, not the trustees, are the owners; but to make up for the failure to focus the relief on the beneficiaries we are treated to detailed pages of academic discussion on implied trusts and estoppel just to show HMRC is aware of it. The guidance gives us HMRC's view on principles of beneficial ownership following legal ownership in the absence of evidence to the contrary – citing Lady Hale and Lord Walker in *Stack v. Dowden*.[67] We are taken[68] through the various ingredients for a common intention constructive trust with Lord Browne-Wilkinson's judgement in *Grant v. Edwards*[69] as a guide as cited in *Oxley v. Hiscock*; right the way through to the relationship between constructive trusts and proprietary estoppel,[70] he points out that the two concepts are very similar (see above).

Reading through the guidance on common intention constructive trusts raises some questions. In a constructive trust scenario, it is usually the down-trodden and ignored beneficiary trying to argue there is a trust such that a beneficial and proprietary claim over the disputed property arises. Most of the cases concerning constructive trusts and proprietary estoppel do not

---

[64][2004] EWCA Civ 524

[65][2007] 2 AC 432 (HL)

[66]HMRC Guidance CG65420

[67]HMRC Guidance CG65421

[68]HMRC Guidance CG65422 onwards

[69][1986] EWCA Civ 4

[70]HMRC Guidance CG65430

concern tax, rather about having a stake in a property; they are unlikely to argue they have a stake purely so they can pay HMRC some income tax or CGT. But in HMRC's guidance the whole focus is about *the trustees'* arguing that there is a trust, that there is a downtrodden and ignored beneficiary so that they might be able to claim this relief through s.225 even though they don't occupy the property themselves. In the section about quantifying the beneficial interest, HMRC's guidance states:[71]

> *"When applied to TCGA92/S225 this means that the legal owners of the property will claim they held the property as trustees of a constructive trust under which a person occupies the property as a beneficiary of that trust. The legal owners will also be the settlors of the trust as they will have provided the property either by buying it so it can be occupied or by providing a property they already own. The terms of the trust will usually be that the beneficiary had a life interest in the property"*

Why is everything so back-to-front with PPR? The main reason is because of the wording of TCGA 1992 s.225 which places the emphasis squarely on the trustee. When TCGA 1992 s.68 talks about 'settled property' they mean it in the same way as the IHT legislation which means an actual express trust structure (more specifically, a 'qualifying' pre-2006 IIP trust) must be in place. However, with IHT if a property is in your 'settled' estate the beneficiary is deemed to own it albeit via a formal trust structure. However, for PPR, HMRC take the definition of 'settled property' and apply it to implied trusts as well as express ones. They don't accept the concept that a beneficial owner might be the actual true owner by virtue of an implied trust. In general, as per TCGA 1992 s.1, the beneficial owner is the centre of attention; it seems this is not the case under a settled property structure for PPR.

This is arguably a major misalignment. The person who is chargeable on the tax should also be the one who can claim the relief – that is a fundamental concept within UK tax law. Under TCGA 1992 s.1, we are saying that the beneficial owner of an asset is subject to CGT; but if that asset is a main residence within an express or implied trust (but not a nominee arrangement) then it is the trustee as legal owner who would receive the benefit of PPR. That is not normally an issue with an express trust, whereby the trustee is liable for the CGT. But in an implied trust, if a property were to be sold, the beneficial owner would be assessable to tax ordinarily; but if

---

[71]HMRC Guidance CG65422

the property qualifies as a main residence (for someone) it is the legal owner who would assume the tax burden and claim the relief.

This misalignment does not, however, spread as far as income tax. In an implied trust arrangement, the beneficial owner would face that burden. The trustees would only pay the tax if it were a formal express trust – they would not shift the burden onto an implied trustee as the income tax stays with the beneficial owner:

> "Taxation of income is based on beneficial ownership, not legal ownership"[72]

This oddity with CGT and PPR is purely down to the definitions contained in TCGA 1992 s.225 and s.68.

8.2.2.2   CGT and the Courts

In the section above, we looked at some detail into PPR, in particular the relationship between the legal and beneficial owner within a formal express trust. The statute only seems to recognise actual beneficial ownership through an express trust structure with settled assets. However, if no trust were there, and the asset were therefore not a settled one under TCGA, the same principles surrounding beneficial ownership would apply to CGT – including PPR.

A FTT case to illustrate the imposition of an implied trust within a straightforward CGT situation is that of *Lawson v. HMRC.*[73] This case was in many respects a very simple one. Yvonne Lawson was the legal owner of the property, but the issue was purely whether she was the beneficial owner as well. *Stack v. Dowden*[74] tells us that the default position is that the legal owner is also the beneficial owner, unless any evidence is produced to the contrary, and this was at the heart of this case. HMRC believed that, as sole legal owner, Mrs Lawson was also the sole beneficial owner. Mrs Lawson contended that her husband was joint beneficial owner and thus jointly liable for the CGT upon eventual sale. When the property was bought, the couple already had their main residence in the husband's name, so it was felt best for the property to be bought in the wife's name; however, the husband was contributing 80-90% toward the mortgage on the new house. The house was lived in by their daughter whilst at university and she contributed nominal amounts toward the costs, all of which went into the wife's bank account,

---

[72]HMRC Guidance TSEM9305

[73][2011] UKFTT 346 (TC)

[74][2007] 2 AC 432 (HL)

mainly because the husband only had one (sole trader) account. More importantly, the deposit on the purchase of the house came largely from the couple's savings and an inheritance the wife had received – the bulk of the savings came from an endowment policy held by the husband. The FTT therefore had no hesitation in holding that the house was in joint beneficial ownership and so the resulting trust was imposed on the basis of the contributions and the mortgage payments, as well as the nature of the purchase in the first place i.e. buying somewhere for their daughter to live rather than as a commercial investment.

This example is a classic resulting trust case – the concept stated by Eyre CB in *Dyer v. Dyer* could be applied directly to this case; indeed it was, and by an administrative tax tribunal.

8.3   Examples of 'pure equity' besides trusts

Implied trusts are a product of the principles of equity, but they are not the only tools which the courts can use to implement what is fair and just. Since their earliest days, the courts have been able to do whatever they think is necessary to correct a rigid or unjust law. This section examines two instances where the tax courts have done just that. Neither of the two cases below focuses on capital income, nor looks at the intricate differences between express/implied or resulting/constructive trusts. In these two cases the courts used pure equity to right two wrongs. As far as common law was concerned, HMRC were perfectly justified in demanding tax from these individuals and there were no real legal arguments to be made in their defence. However, in both instances, purely equitable principles saw HMRC's assessments being dismissed. More importantly, both of them were heard in the FTT – the court of first instance for appeal against HMRC assessments.

The first example concerns an equitable remedy now known and legislated for as 'Special Relief'.[75]

Example 1: *John Clark v. HMRC*[76]

John Clark suffered from severe learning difficulties with a mental age of 12 and his wife registered him for self-assessment income tax as a self-employed painter and decorator. She also took care of his paperwork, but she subsequently left him in March 2003 and eventually died, leaving him to look after their daughter. Given the understandable depression which

---

[75]From April 2011 contained within Para 3A Schedule 1AB Taxes Management Act (TMA) 1970
[76] July 2015 (FTT)

followed, he failed to complete his tax returns from then until 2013 when he found labouring work which was subject to PAYE. He later tried to communicate with HMRC with a letter (which his daughter wrote, but which HMRC returned) and he visited their offices three times, but they were unable to communicate with him as they did not appreciate his learning difficulties. Following his failure to submit income tax returns despite Notices to File being issued, HMRC issued six years' worth of Determination notices, making their own estimated assessments totalling nearly £18,000.

Prior to 1 April 2011, Special Relief was an extra-statutory equitable relief. Once enshrined in law, it may be used by individuals and limited companies when faced with an HMRC Determination assessment. The criteria are that, as well as having one's affairs otherwise up to date and Special Relief (or pre-2011 equitable equivalent) has not been used before, it would be unconscionable for HMRC to seek to recover the amount which has been charged by a determination or refuse to repay it if it has already been paid. 'Unconscionable' obviously has its roots deep within the history of equity – the law of conscience.

Having made this Special Relief claim in the face of these Determinations, John Clark faced opposition from HMRC who argued that their Determinations were not unconscionable, that Mr Clark had been given plenty of time to respond, and a timely submission of his returns would have superseded the Determinations.

When faced with this, the FTT needed to look at the definition of 'unconscionable', which is given no meaning within the TMA 1970. The FTT borrowed the definition used in a similar, earlier case of *William Maxwell*[77] whereby the Judge Alistair Rankin had defined it as *"completely unreasonable"* and *"unreasonably excessive"*.[78] In the present case, the Judge Kenneth Mure added to this definition: *"inordinate or outrageous"*. The conclusion was that:

> *"Accordingly, the question of whether it was unconscionable for the respondents to refuse the appellant's claim is to be considered against a known background of the appellant's dyslexia, his general learning difficulties, his reliance on other family members in the absence of his wife,*

---

[77]*William Maxwell* TC02849 August 2013 (FTT) – in that case the appellant, also of limited education had relied solely on his accountant who had died

[78]Also described as such in HMRC Guidance SACM12240

and the probable destruction of much of the relevant notifications from HMRC...

HMRC's response to the letter of June 2011 and at the interviews shortly after were inadequate and unsatisfactory given the appellant's personal difficulties. A further distinction in relation to these other matters is that the appellant was aware of there being a "live" issue. However, he did not appreciate the urgency and significance of the dispute with HMRC. We appreciate that at the interview when the tax officer spelled out the words of the response, only one – possibly inexperienced – officer was present. But it was an opportunity which should have at least alerted HMRC to the peculiar circumstances of this case...

Full information as to the appellant's condition and circumstances was made available. Notwithstanding the respondents still refuse the claim. The appellant appears to have been fully cooperative at all material times. Given that context we consider that the respondents' refusal of the claim was unreasonable".[79]

The appeal was therefore allowed and the determinations were set aside. This case revolved predominately around whether it would have been 'unconscionable' for HMRC to enforce the Determinations. HMRC were not wrong in issuing them; John Clark had failed to respond to Notices to File tax returns and so HMRC were obliged to estimate the income and make their own assessments. But, in these specific circumstances, this would have been morally wrong, inequitable. It is for these types of scenario that the equity courts were established in the first place, all those centuries ago. The appellant has no claim under common law; the defendant, in this case HMRC, had done nothing legally wrong, but a breach of equity had taken place and so the FTT, a humble, first instance tax court intervened. That is pure equity demonstrated by our modern tax courts.

According to HMRC, this Special Relief would usually only be allowed where *"a person is considered vulnerable, has not received our notices or other communications for reasons outside their control or is insolvent".[80]* When deciding whether is someone is vulnerable HMRC would look to ascertain:

"what is the nature of their condition? does it affect their ability to manage their tax affairs - if so, how? does it affect their ability to deal or communicate with HMRC - if so, how? does anyone help them manage their tax affairs,

---

[79]TC04509 para 30-31

[80]HMRC Guidance SACM12240

such as a family member, friend or agent - if so, what arrangements are in place for this person to deal with HMRC on their behalf?[81]"

Example 2: *Rebecca Vowles v. HMRC*[82]

This case also concerned income tax assessments issued by HMRC (more specifically a fraud investigation under COP9), concerning dividends and benefits-in-kind from a company of which Ms Vowles was sole shareholder and director. Once again, HMRC were (legally) absolutely right to do so. On the face of it, Ms Vowles failed to declare this income when asked to do so and thus legally had few avenues for counterargument. Despite having her own business to run, she was the shareholder of the limited company which paid the dividends and was also the director for whom a company car was 'made available'.

Behind the scenes and the façade which common law would exclusively observe, there was an abusive relationship. Her partner physically and mentally abused her, the judge summarised:[83]

"He mentally abused her by denigrating her: he would criticise her personal appearance and ignore her. He would always put her down verbally. Their relationship was a cycle of abuse followed by making up"....

"He controlled her finances. Around the time she became pregnant with their first child in 2005, he persuaded her to give him control of her bank cards. Thereafter, he would then only permit her to access her bank accounts when he decided and only for purchases he dictated....

Mr Walker (her partner) did not permit Ms Vowles to write letters; he controlled her correspondence with HMRC although she accepts that she may well have signed the letters sent to HMRC, as she signed what was put in front of her. Any letters which arrived at their home, even if addressed to her, were left for Mr Walker to open....

Physical abuse commenced in 2005, about 18 months after their relationship began and around the time she became pregnant. Mr Walker (her partner) would spit at her and physically push her around. He once locked her in the jacuzzi with little air and she passed out. On another occasion, he hit her head against a wall, causing her to lose consciousness, yet she told the ambulance crew that she had had a panic attack. He broke her foot and collar bone."

---

[81]HMRC Guidance SACM12245

[82]TC06123 September 2017 (FTT)

[83]Barbara Mosedale, paragraphs 16-20

IMPLIED TRUSTS

The company in issue was set up by Ms Vowles because her partner was disqualified as a director, so she took on the role as director and shareholder as a figurehead for him. The company was later investigated for fraud and liquidated. Whilst she was the owner with all the relevant responsibilities in law, it was the partner who ran it; she did whatever he said and signed whatever he told her to sign (indeed, he would forge her signature to sign her up to liabilities such as loans and re-mortgages). In reality, she had nothing to do with the company, could not read the post addressed to her, had no idea about the dividends or loans and had no access to the company's bank account. The judge pointed out again that the common law was not on Ms Vowles's side, and, despite all the facts pointing to her not being liable, there were no legal grounds to strike down HMRC's enquiries and resulting assessments:

> *"While we accept that she was the victim in an abusive relationship, and in practice did not know the contents of the tax returns nor read the post sent to her, we consider that as a matter of law she would have to show duress in the sense of fear of imminent danger in order to vitiate her consent to Mr Walker acting on her behalf in completing her tax returns, reading her post, and corresponding with HMRC. We make this finding of law on the basis of an analogy with the law of contract[84]."*

Therefore, HMRC's enquiry was valid in common law. However, despite HMRC's submissions that Ms Vowles must have known what was going on within the company, the FTT did not accept that argument. As far as the ownership of the company is concerned:

> *"We have accepted Ms Vowles account that she was unaware that she was the shareholder of Nettex (the limited company in question) and in any event, that she understood that so far as she was concerned, she was a mere figurehead in respect of the company, which was in reality Mr Walker's company. He ran the company, controlled its finances and spent its profits, whether lawfully or unlawfully obtained, while Ms Vowles did not have access to the company's funds save to the extent Mr Walker permitted her to spend money[85]".*

However, the most significant passages were as follows[86] and critical words and sentences are numbered:

---

[84]Paragraph 57

[85]Paragraph 83

[86]Paragraphs 84-86

"Our finding is that while in law she was the shareholder, in equity (1) it is clear that she held that share on trust for Mr Walker, even though neither party, not being lawyers, would have thought about the matter using such terminology (2). But the situation Ms Vowles described was clearly one where her name was used, but she had no beneficial interest in the company…

We do not consider her the beneficial owner of the share in her name…

In conclusion, it was clearly Mr Walker to whom the dividend was paid. He controlled the director's loan account and the dividend was credited to the director's loan account. Further, the dividends were clearly received by Mr Walker. He controlled the company's bank accounts and decided how the profits should be spent (including in 2008 making a few direct payments into Ms Vowles's account albeit at a time when he had possession of her bank cards). Ms Vowles did not have access to the company bank accounts and did not receive the dividends. Lastly, Ms Vowles was not entitled to receive the dividends because she held her share on behalf of Mr Walker, who was in equity the person entitled to receive the dividends.

In short, we find that Ms Vowles was not the person liable for the tax on the dividends. While we think s 385 must be read as giving liability to a single person, in any event our finding is that whichever test in s 385 is applied, Ms Vowles was not the person liable to the tax. The dividend was not paid to her, it was not received by her and she was not in equity entitled to it (3)".

Once again, these few paragraphs sum up pure equity. To break them down:

Point 1: The FTT, a first instance tax court, used the word 'equity', having earlier distinguished the legal position.

Point 2: The implied trust element is highlighted by these words. The share of which Ms Vowles was the legal owner was actually held in the capacity of a trustee. Her partner was the real beneficial owner. The point about neither party's using such terminology is reminiscent of Lord Halsbury LC's words in *Smith v. Cooke* about *"putting in words which are not there".*

Point 3: We noted above the legal position regarding the receipt of dividends which echoes what the judge says here about ITTOIA 2005 s.385. HMRC's position that Ms Vowles, as the legal shareholder, was entitled to and received the dividend would seem valid. But in the circumstances, in the facts behind the legal assumption, equity deemed that Ms Vowles was neither entitled to nor received those dividends and so should not be taxed on them. The FTT took the relatively simple statutory definition and viewed it through a prism of equity; again, using the words 'in equity'.

There was a company car too, which HMRC assessed upon Ms Vowles on the basis that her employer (the company) had made the car available for Ms Vowles's private use as a director. However, given the circumstances already outlined, the FTT held that as a matter of fact, the company had made the car available to her partner, who had subsequently given Ms Vowles use of the car. HMRC's assessment on that benefit was set aside. As with the dividends, a simple statutory definition – in this case being 'made available' – was viewed through the same prism of equity because the facts simply did match the common law legal presumption.

9 Conclusion

"It is a weary word this Chancery!" [1]

In many respects beneficial ownership is a fiction - a fiction which is called into existence purely by good conscience and natural justice. Ever since our law began to develop in medieval days following the inception of a common law, equity has been a guiding thread to ensure that natural justice is done. The legal ownership is the only official one, the one written down – that is the true and official ownership, but that is not the same as being the rightful owner. It is in equity whence this fiction arose; the legislation grants the existence of beneficial ownership (as well as the prevalence of equity), HMRC recognises it, as do the courts using the tool of implied trusts using their inherent equitable jurisdiction.

Aside from the settlements and TOAA legislation, the income tax legislation also recognises the beneficial, not legal, ownership of income and assets, albeit more recently and in a more ambiguous and open-minded way. IHT and CGT legislation recognised beneficial ownership early on; IR and HMRC, as government agencies, also acknowledge the importance of beneficial ownership through their own guidance to their inspectors and staff. However, this guidance has itself come from HMRC's recognition and interpretation of principles founded by the equity courts over the years. So, as well as equity growing from within the courts system, it has found its way into the executive.

Despite the legislator's relatively slow recognition of equitable ownership within income tax, the settlements and TOAA legislation are good examples of the legislator's specifically imposing a (settlor-interested) implied trust early on. However, this legislation was introduced because of a specific problem i.e. artificial income-shifting. This statutory implied trust therefore did not have to evolve from the centuries of development of equity; it has a long pedigree within its own statute which has remained virtually unchanged in nearly one hundred years and has been the subject of cases throughout the highest courts in the land. The legislation raises wider questions about tax and the family unit in the UK with the exemption for gifts of capital assets only applying to spouses/civil partners, when fewer and fewer households are married ones. In addition, but related to that, is the fact that the imposition of a settlor-interested implied trust by the legislation runs counter to the principle of individual assessment. It re-

---

[1] Charles Dickens, *Bleak House*, chapter 5

imposes the old system of aggregation in the case of a spouse gifting sources of income which goes against the notions of equality which prompted the change in 1990; so, it is arguably a retrograde step in matters of women's equality, as it is usually the husband who is the deemed settlor as in *Arctic Systems*.

When asking how beneficial ownership is the foundation of modern UK tax law, the answer is that beneficial ownership (and the equitable principles which allowed implied trusts to impose such ownership) was within the courts long before direct taxation existed. Such trusts influenced the courts which had developed and grown around equity from their initial creation. Statutory acknowledgement of equity's preferential status was confirmed with the 1873 Act.

The 2009 reforms were significant in restructuring all the government tribunals, not just those for tax, but the change was also an interesting symbolic one by the effective placing of the old Special Commissioners into the Chancery Division of the High Court. The new UT is now essentially the Chancery Division of the High Court as far as tax law is concerned – the appellate tax tribunal has now immersed itself within the home of equity and has embraced its principles – including beneficial interests and implied trusts. The tax courts are now effectively unified with the equity courts. So, it was the tax courts which found their way into equitable principles more than the other way around: the jurisdiction of the Exchequer of Pleas, the transfer of that jurisdiction into the Chancery Division in 1880 and finally the Chancery Division's effective metamorphosis into the UT. It is all intertwined; the growth of equity within the first tax court in the land and the jurisdiction of tax law were swept up with the development of equity.

As a result of this, HMRC are obviously duty bound to follow this trend and conduct their enforcement transactions through the prism of beneficial ownership.

If one were to ask 'to what extent' is beneficial ownership the foundation of UK tax law, the answer is that beneficial ownership is the cornerstone of modern UK taxation; it is engrained in the whole system. It takes priority over legal ownership for tax purposes in conjunction with the prevalence of equity over law and is the basis on which tax in the UK operates and determines ownership of an income source or asset. HMRC make this clear throughout their manuals, the legislation is now liberally scattered with reference to ownership's being beneficial and the courts have long since enforced such ownership. In these days of greater awareness of likely money-laundering risks, identifying beneficial ownership is more important than ever; the advent of 5AMLD and the tightening of the Trust Registration Service compliance requirements is a good indicator of this new climate.

Whilst beneficial ownership may be a fiction in some respect, is not a mere concept either; a beneficial owner is a real person and has always been there, but the official acknowledgement of his existence has been led by the equity courts' turning it from a fiction into something more tangible, more real. Initially, only these courts recognised that legal owner's existence. As the influence of equity increased (and the legislation placed their jurisdiction in a position of primacy), and with its imposition through targeted statute and implied trusts, beneficial ownership became 'mainstream' and was recognised as such by the executive. In particular, the income tax laws were born and grew up as equity was nearing its zenith. Whilst the income tax legislation was generally slow to distinguish between legal and beneficial owners, the settlements legislation and that for TOAA recognised the 'real' owner of a source of income. However, for tax purposes generally, these trusts are called 'bare trusts'. It is of little concern to them how the beneficial ownership came to be split away from the legal owner, whether it is due to the settlements or TOAA legislation or any other reason. The words 'implied', 'resulting' or 'constructive' trusts are rarely used by HMRC, the tax legislation or the courts and tribunals. Those terms, along with the stories of how and why the trusts came about, tend to belong in the lawyers' books.

Whatever you call those trusts and however you interpret their role, the ancient legal institutions of the UK and good conscience created them. These same institutions now create, enforce and interpret the UK's tax law through the prism of long-established equity. The basis of taxation in the UK is beneficial ownership, manifested through one of equity's greatest creations – the implied trust.

Bibliography

Books

Baker, Sir John. *Introduction to English Legal History* (Oxford University Press, 2018)

Banks, R. *Lindley & Banks on Partnership* (Sweet & Maxwell, 20th Edition, 2017)

Birks, P. *Restitution & Equity Volume 1: Resulting Trusts and Equitable Compensation* (London Mansfield Press, 2000)

Bryson, W H. *Cases concerning equity 1550-1660: Volume 1* (Seldon Society, 2001)

Bryson, W H. *The Equity Side of the Exchequer* (Cambridge University Press, 1975)

Chambers, R. *Resulting Trusts* (Clarendon Press, 1997)

Hayton, D and others, *Underhill & Hayton Law of Trusts & Trustees* (Lexis Nexis, 19th Edition, 2017)

Holdsworth, Sir William. *A History of English Law: Volume 1* (Sweet & Maxwell, 7th Edition, 1956)

Hudson, J. *The Oxford History of the Laws of England (Volume 11 1820-1914)* (Oxford University Press, 2012)

Loutzenhiser, G. *Tiley's Revenue Law* (Hart Publishing, 9th Edition, 2019)

Millet, P J. *Unjust Enrichment* (Oxford University Press, 2nd Edition, 2004)

Mitchell, C. *Constructive & Resulting Trusts* (Oxford Hart, 2010)

Oliver, D & Harris, P, *Comparative Perspectives on Revenue Law* (Cambridge University Press, 2008)

Waters, D. *The Constructive Trust: the case for a new approach to English Law* (University of London Press, 1964)

Articles

Chartered Institute of Taxation, *Couples in the tax and related welfare systems – a call for greater clarity* (May 2015)

Craggs, A. "A step too far?" (*Trust and Estate Law & Tax Journal*, January/February 2011)

Millett, P J. *Restitution & Constructive Trusts* (1998) LJR 399

Oliver, D & Harris P. *Comparative perspectives on revenue law* (Cambridge University Press, 2008)

Stopford, D. *Settlement and the avoidance of tax on income* (BTR 1990, 7, 225)

Tiley, J. *Tax, marriage and the family* (CJL 2006, 65(2), 289)

BIBLIOGRAPHY

(Radcliffe) Royal Commission on the Taxation of Profits and Income, Final Report, 1955

Colwyn Committee and the Incidence of Income Tax, 1928

Canadian Royal Commission on Tax, 1966

Royal Commission on The Income Tax, 1919-1920

Index

www.ingramcontent.com/pod-product-compliance
Lightning Source LLC
Chambersburg PA
CBHW070738220326
41598CB00024BA/3464